Brouhaha

Worlds of the Contemporary

Lionel Ruffel

Translated by
Raymond N. MacKenzie

A Univocal Book

University of Minnesota Press
Minneapolis · London

The University of Minnesota Press gratefully acknowledges financial support for the publication of this book from le Centre national du livre.

The University of Minnesota Press acknowledges the contribution of Jason Wagner, Univocal's publisher, in making this volume possible.

Originally published in French as *Brouhaha* in 2016; copyright 2016 by Éditions Verdier.

Published by the University of Minnesota Press
111 Third Avenue South, Suite 290
Minneapolis, MN 55401-2520
http://www.upress.umn.edu

ISBN 978-1-5179-0488-3

A Cataloging-in-Publication record for this book is available from the Library of Congress.

Printed in the United States of America on acid-free paper

The University of Minnesota is an equal-opportunity educator and employer.

22 21 20 19 18   10 9 8 7 6 5 4 3 2

Contents

Introduction

What is the contemporary? For about ten years now, this question has traveled and traversed a number of cultures and languages. First, in 2004, it emerged in the form "*¿Qué es lo contemporaneo?*" as a series of articles published in the Argentinian magazine *Zum*, from the Centro de Expresiones Contemporáneas de Rosario. Then the question popped up again in Venice, with Giorgio Agamben asking, *Che cos'è il contemporaneo?* After that, twice in France: in Rouen, several architects explored the question, followed by literary scholars and philosophers in Pantin. The question of the contemporary then found its way back to Italy, associated with a performing arts event; then we find it again, in 2011, in Santiago, Chile, in a book that brought together historians, philosophers, and cultural studies specialists; and then in Brussels, within the elegant interdisciplinary journal *Pylône*. Once Agamben's book was translated, the question appeared in English, and in 2012, Stanford University asked in three languages, "*O que é contemporaneo?*" "*Qué es lo contemporaneo?*" and "*What is the contemporary?*" Not until 2014, way up north at St. Andrews in Scotland, was the question posed in English alone. In the meantime—from 2009 to 2012—this apparent preoccupation of an era went through a number of variations, most notably in the form of a questionnaire titled "The Contemporary," which traveled

1

throughout the entire art world and was taken up again and again, revised, augmented, and attacked from New York to Hong Kong, while passing through Berlin to New Delhi. And most recently, a journal issue dedicated to "Contemporâneo Hoje" kept the debate alive in São Paulo.[1]

A great diversity of worlds found themselves reflected, separately and mutually, through this word that seems to denote, if not the formation of a historical identity (something diversity no longer really permits), then at least a common preoccupation with ideas, however conflicting, about time, history, and space regarding how to live within them and how to form both subjectivities and communities, and ideas about representations, technologies, and imaginaries. Many other words have had the same fate, becoming key signifiers for how a community will designate itself. The fact that the word *contemporary* has joined the majestic list of historical–aesthetic categories (like *Modernity, Renaissance, Enlightenment*) ought to attract our attention, especially since the word is used—even more than its shiny precursors—as a self-designated category in all the domains of our common life and in every field of (media, domestic, professional, disciplinary, political, and artistic) discourse, and also—this is a first—to refer to the entirety of the planet.

This totalization raises some questions. It arises, no doubt, from the primary sense of the word *contemporary* ("of or belonging to the same time"), which is transitive or, rather, relational ("belonging to the same time *as . . .*"). To share the same time assumes (in whatever forms) to share a space, an imaginary, a history—to form a common body. Carrying no meanings beyond the relational one (unlike, say, *Renaissance*), the word *contemporary* is doubly a historical marker, a word by which groups refer to themselves and by which they see themselves as groups. In this sense, it overspills its "epoch," "our epoch," to refer to any process of constituting a collective based on a shared space-time. It's a doubly significant key word, then, but also a meta-word belonging to historical consciousness that, for that reason, can hold contradictory meanings as well as open up a significant moment for reflection.

For a decade or so now, we've been experimenting with this reflection that, for the second time, has changed the grammatical and semantic nature of the word. For several centuries, *contemporary* simply meant co-presence in a passing moment of time, condemned to transience, to signifying nothing more than a present moment reduced to the ephemeral; after the Second World War, the term began to be used to designate the era, though discreetly and usually as an adjective, set aside from noisier debates (such as discussions on the postmodern). It has only been very recently that the word has become a substantive and, consequently, has increased in substance to become *the* contemporary, charged with multiple meanings. And the more it became *the* contemporary, in the singular, the more those meanings proliferated.

Having observed this substantivation, this deployment as a noun, in various localized forms over several years, what strikes me is this combination of unity and diversity: the unity of the designation itself and the diversity of its meanings. And instead of collapsing under the hailstorm of so many meanings, the word is even more consistently applied, as if it received its full meaning only through endless disputes. So one can understand the logic behind why a meta-word such as the contemporary imposes itself as a marker for our era. Sharing doesn't mean agreement or consensus, at least not always. Sharing means taking part, participating. My hypothesis is that this meta-word of sharing and relation has become so prevalent because those who do take part or share in this same era have never been so numerous and so diverse (and, more importantly, so conscious of being so), and they have probably never been less in agreement. Each inhabits his or her own era, his or her own conception of the era, his or her own temporality. So much so that "being of the same time" seems more like a synchronization of multiple temporalities, a kind of *co*-temporality.

And so it's difficult, at this point, to present a univocal, coherent vision of the contemporary. And so, here begins a lengthy inquiry, starting with the need to withdraw from the epistemological modes of the modern, and especially from an a priori position that orients everything to our historical moment. This position can be concisely formulated: the contemporary is simply the new modern. This would entail at least two things: first, that the contemporary would present itself as something new in relation to a previous state; second, that it is one historical sequence substituting itself for another (for, in the imaginary of the modern, every historical sequence is always being succeeded by another). But this way of thinking—in which the modern representation of historical temporality (sequential and successive) is in fact what historical temporality actually *is*—is precisely what the contemporary calls into question. The very meaning of *contemporary*, both as a word (assuming composition, organization, and nonseparation or sameness) and as a mode of being in time, denotes *not* replicating the modern understanding of historical temporality.

THE AESTHETIC HYPOTHESIS: THE CONTEMPORARY AS NEW MODERN

To get a better grip on the modern approach to historical temporality, we can draw out its logic. The term *contemporary* has, for a good half a century, been used in a series of expressions: "contemporary literature," "contemporary dance," "contemporary art," "contemporary music," "contemporary architecture," along with other phrases that have modified the word's nature and lexical universe. In this series, *contemporary* effects the convergence of a number of practices that happen to be artistic ones, and it effects this convergence under the phenomenon of historical temporality. Moreover, the series implicitly puts *contemporary* in dialogue with other ideas (ancient, classical, modern) whose meanings aren't always clearly defined but are at least familiar. And they are familiar as belonging to a class of specific words denoting aesthetic–historical categories. First aesthetic, and then historical, since the ones in question operate in the aesthetic field as historical categories. So we can begin by investigating the contemporary as an aesthetic category, which, as we shall see, also means to investigate its relation to the modern and to modernity.

Since we begin by positing a duality—duality, that automatic reflex of thought—this duality of modern–contemporary, let's turn to a text that is one of the most pointed analyses of the modern, which will provide us with a matrix for our analysis of aesthetic categories. This text, well known to literary scholars, is by Hans Robert Jauss, on the appearance and metamorphoses of the term *modernity*.[2] I want to explore Jauss's idea that there is such a thing as a historical consciousness, one that is variable or relative to the present and more or less intense, and that moments of great intensity are characterized by the formation or the reactivation of a word. The degree of intensity can be measured (Jauss does not specify this, but we can infer from his study) by the use or reactivation of a word relevant to temporality, like *ancient, Renaissance, modern, modernity*. According to Jauss, such moments are relatively rare. They signal the formation of a historical identity, that is, a moment in which the relationship between aesthetic experience, political experience, and historical experience becomes crystallized in a word. *Contemporary* corresponds to all his criteria. Constructed using a word related to historical temporality, it signals a moment of great intensity in the historical awareness of the present. But none of that explains why "the contemporary" is emerging, nor why it's becoming dominant.

Following Jauss's example, we can pause first on the history of the word *contemporary,* recalling that not only in French but in most Latin languages, as well as in English, its extended usage is a recent phenomenon. Arising from its Latin form *contemporaneus,* "of the same time," the word appeared in its current French form *(contemporain)* in the fifteenth century, and then underwent three expansions of usage, corresponding to three moments of aesthetic and philosophical crisis in Europe (i.e., the Renaissance, the "*querelle des anciens et des modernes*," and the Enlightenment). Even so, its usage remained limited, as did its range and meaning, primarily because a much older word, one much more traditional in a sense and much more semantically charged, was preferred: *modern.* Thus *modern* has always designated the newness given us by a present, in relation to *antiquitas.*[3]

We must therefore try to understand why *modern* is less used today, while *contemporary* has pervaded our discourse on the representation of the historical present. To analyze changes of aesthetic category, Jauss suggests we examine linguistic usage alongside aesthetic and historical experience. Because the word *contemporary* has become more consistently used and has emerged as a key concept since the Second World War, we can deduce that this disruption of *modern* in favor of *contemporary* is connected to the profound changes that were taking place in the world at that time. Four of these are especially remarkable for what this new obsession with the word *contemporary* might mean.

The first parameter is at once demographic, political, and cultural. After the Second World War, the West, possessor of both economic and symbolic capital, saw an unprecedented demographic event, the famous baby boom, which resulted in a democratization of and greatly increased access to knowledge, culture, and emancipation by way of creation. Preferring experience and practice to erudition and scholarship, a new generation inexorably came to power and sought a new name for itself, something denoting its difference. At the same time, the world's cultural and intellectual map was modified and decentered, first recentering itself on the other side of the Atlantic, and then, more recently, "multicentering" itself, particularly in the postcolonial "period." Hitherto invisible artists and intellectuals emerged out of previously dominated regions, suggesting an image of the present that the already overused word *modernity* would no longer fit. More importantly, this image of the present contested many of the main aspects of modernity, especially its Eurocentrism and, more generally, its tendency to privilege the majority over the minority.

At the same time, there occurred both a war of sorts *and* a *querelle,* without which a new epoch would not have made itself and its difference visible. In the early 1980s, in the United States, the canon wars broke out, demonstrating how every tradition is constructed, every community imaginary—especially national traditions and communities. The teaching of literature and "great books" had formed one of the essential pillars of that nation-centered kind of education that characterizes modernity. We now work in the aftermath of its demolition, which introduced contemporary cultural objects of study into scholarly and university life.

As for the *querelle,* this concerned "contemporary art." Twenty years later, what is left? An impassioned series of questions about the structuring of artistic space: what to show, where to show it, for what audience, and for what relation among artist, organizer, and those who enter the exhibition space? Reflections on contemporary art—especially those initiated by artists and their proposals—served as inspirations in other cultural fields, for they spoke perfectly to this new demographic, political, and cultural mutation.

From the point of view of historical temporality, then, and uniquely from that point of view—problematic as it so evidently is—we can put together a more or less coherent sequence of events that led to this recourse to the new term. This moment of the contemporary, born in the second half of the twentieth century, is largely characterized by its usage of the word *contemporary* to name itself, though its definition remains rather elusive. But far from being meaningless, the word marks a series of important transformations that develop certain principles of modernity without rejecting, at least not apparently, the foundations of modern consciousness.

If they do not reject those foundations, it is because, contrary to what one might think at first, *modern* and *contemporary* are not situated on the same plane and thus are not in opposition to each other. According to Jauss, ever since the end of the Roman Empire, historical consciousness has been structured by an opposition between the old and the new, or rather between the old and the modern. The old and the modern vary with the times, as does the nature of the opposition between them. Sometimes they take form within a series of words that constitute a second level in the historical representation of the present. On one side, one might find *ancient* or *classical*; on the other, variations include *modernity* or *modernism* or even, and Jauss's essay is significant in this regard, *romanticism*. A third level would be made up of artistic movements or political tendencies. The aesthetic hypothesis maintains that *contemporary* is a term of the second level, entirely comparable with *romanticism* or *modernity,* for example, as Jauss's analysis suggests. In this sense, the contemporary would be a form of the modern, like the Renaissance, romanticism, or modernity. The point seems irrefutable.

DOUBTS ABOUT THE AESTHETIC HYPOTHESIS

However, no one puts it so explicitly. On the contrary, the point is often in doubt, because it revives a highly debated mode of understanding aesthetic–historical categories, the mode frequently termed "epochal."[4] In this sense, the contemporary would be an epoch, and in fact "our" epoch, since only ours claims it as a criterion of our collective identification. Now, this "our" is problematic. The "contemporary" world (in the epochal sense) is marked by so many diverse and contradictory realities as to practically invalidate the possibility of an "our." This all-encompassing "our" cannot be spoken about without harboring either some sort of imperialism or egocentrism. Imperialism, because the "our" requires bringing the entirety of all collective phenomena together into a geographically and temporally situated representation. And egocentrism, because the ensemble of these collective phenomena must be situated in relation to the person speaking. And this is why a great deal of cultural and aesthetic critique was only capable of glimpsing major phenomena or ruptures, simply because that critique itself participates in them.

At the same time, from an epistemological point of view, the epochal approach poses the problem of periodization and thus a representation with temporal borders. But a particular example should encourage us to distrust periodization: the discipline of history. This discipline, which is not a minor historical discipline since it's the discipline of history itself, has made use of the category of the contemporary more widely than other disciplines. In the traditional representation it uses for historical time (subject to numerous and already very long-standing internal critiques), it presents four large-scale periods: ancient history, medieval history, modern history, and contemporary history. Now the latter poses the problems of borders. Where does it begin? Where does it end? For that matter, does it end? Among all the solutions proposed, none is very good. On one hand, since the automatic reflex has been to stick to national histories, the beginning of the contemporary period can be considered 1789, or 1914, or 1917, or 1945. Here again we encounter that familiar egocentrism and imperialism. On the other hand, another reflex has been to stick to "major events." Now, every contemporary historiography has critiqued this approach, including literary history and the history of art, which have very forcefully relativized and problematized a history based on "great works" or "great authors." These ideas—great events, great works—bring us back to the well-known manner of understanding history as so many a posteriori constructions. Finally, the question arises as to whether a period can be viewed as ongoing or if it must be defined in terms involving closure. To respond to this, we must bring forward a fifth period, the history of "the present time," which, even if it does problematize the entire sequence, is not really separate from it. One consequence is that if we follow the example of history, the contemporary period belongs to the past. Another consequence: this model has not been structured for all disciplines, and none of the human or social sciences has really used it. So we must throw out the type of sequentiality that assumes a homogeneity of the epoch, because the epochal approach, so firmly anchored in the history of representations (even in its preceding variants, taking the form of cycles or of ages), however problematized it may have become, still continues to haunt our representation of time and thus of the contemporary.

This critique of sequentiality gives rise to another approach to the contemporary, one that has been strongly privileged in recent years, particularly because it is far more consonant with the very meaning of the word. We can refer to this other method as the *modal* approach. With the modal approach, the contemporary is a relation to historical time, a mode of being in time. It is thus transhistorical. There were as many contemporaries as there were historical moments, each of which was a contemporary in its turn. "Contemporary" thus designates a relation to time, to history, and to what is considered to be current, whatever the epoch one may be referring to. To truly see this point, we need only remind ourselves that any given so-called classical painter was also a contemporary with his time. For this approach, it is more precise to speak of contemporaneity than of the contemporary. The maximalism of this approach may appear troubling. However, the modal approach to the contemporary has something theoretically compelling about it, in the way that it directs us toward unknown lands, nonmodern lands, where history is no longer thought of in terms of epochs. And this is the approach that my study is going to adopt and develop. But I understand that its maximalism may raise fears that it will lead us back into essentialism. To avoid that, we can adjoin to it two other approaches, which we will use as support structures, like a traveler advancing into the unknown using a walking stick. One of these approaches is notional: the contemporary is a notion, and like all notions, it has its own history. And like all histories, we can trace it, provided we think of it as a kind of discourse event. The contemporary is the result of an ensemble of discourses that intersect, respond to each other, superimpose themselves on each other, differentiate themselves from each other. We must be attentive to these discourse events to understand what they mean. The final approach is a subset of the preceding: the institutional approach, a highly visible one. We might think of the institution of the museum, for example, which may have the word "contemporary" engraved in the stone portico above its entrance. The multiplication of such buildings across the entire planet gives us a better idea of how the contemporary has entered our imaginary and what forms it can take.

For the last couple of decades, we have seen an increasingly intense debate concerning the contemporary, which reveals a preoccupation with our historic condition; at the same time, two forms of understanding have emerged: the first, the epochal, returns us to sequentiality and turns the contemporary into a new modern; the second, the modal (nonmodern), contests this historic temporality and sees in the emergence of the word *contemporary* the rise of the modern aesthetic hypothesis. Of course, things are not that unambiguous. And to be fair, one must add that even as the modal approach grows in acceptance, the epochal one remains, at least in the form of a reflex, notably in its notional and institutional variants.

WHAT *CONTEMPORARY* CAN MEAN

The various doubts about the aesthetic hypothesis become reinforced when one takes the time to understand what *contemporary* can mean.

The categories are generally clear enough from their names. To understand them, first we need to know who's speaking. Thus we must distinguish the categories imposed in hindsight by history from those used by the actors themselves: either allo- or auto-definitional. The contemporary is an autodefinitional category, used by the actors themselves. Not always very clearly and not always overtly, but it is nevertheless a category that is used far and wide. In such a case, we are encouraged to think that as an auto-definition, it produces its own meaning. And since these terms, to follow Jauss, have almost always involved temporal vocabulary, our reflex inclines us to think that these categories determine a relation to time.

"With the times," "which is of the same time."

But what does "with the times" mean?

An initial way of understanding "with the times" consists in taking into consideration the question of the present. To be with the times is to be in the present. But what, exactly, is it to be in the present? Eventually, everything depends on the "regime of historicity." One line of inquiry into historiography has long been the semantics of time. For Reinhardt Koselleck first,[5] and then for François Hartog,[6] time is not an empty envelope but rather is filled with subjects who make experience out of it. The articulation between the present and the past, between present and future, is the result of a tension between the field of experience and the horizon of expectation. Following François Hartog, one can distinguish at least three historical regimes—that is, three manners of being in time, according to whether the horizon of expectation is situated in the past (as in myths about the golden age or a lost paradise), in the future (as in the belief in progress and in the new), or in the present. Hartog's argument suggests that a temporal crisis came into being during the twentieth century, and has become radicalized in the twenty-first, so that we are now passing from a substantially futurist regime to a substantially presentist one, for the center of gravity of our time is to be found in the present. Hartog also refers to the "contemporary sense of a permanent, elusive, and almost immobile present, which nevertheless appears to create its own historical time. It is as though," he adds, "there were nothing but the present, like an immense stretch of water endlessly rippling." And he concludes, "'Presentism' is the name I have given to this moment and to today's experience of time."[7]

While the word *presentism,* striking as it is in its historiographic precision, has not made its way into common discourse, I am tempted to adapt Hartog's phrase into my own quasi-tautological proposition: This is the moment, and this is the contemporary experience of the time, that is meant by the word *contemporary.*

Contemporaneity can be understood in a second sense as a co-temporality, as a synchronization of multiple times. During the years I have been exploring the term *contemporary,* I have never failed to encounter it, in works of art and in critical theory as well, as a palimpsestic or layered representation of time, in which the present is not a stage in a sequence but a point of metabolization of all the pasts and all the futures. "Of the same time" refers not to this confraternity of epochs but to a co-temporality in the present of all historical times. Here we come to a Benjaminian vision of history, which is imposed on all the fields of representation and which can help us pinpoint the exact semantics of *contemporary.*

But "with the times" is saying something different. In that *con-* prefix, the Latin *cum-,* there is an accord, an accompaniment, an adhesion that is less apparent in those languages that no longer use it as a preposition or adverb. Another linguistic step or two is needed to see it more clearly. The German is more precise: *Zeitgenössisch,* "contemporary," brings together *Zeit* and *Genosse,* "time" and "partnership" or "camaraderie."[8] To be a "comrade" or a "companion in time" is a problematic concept, often mocked in theoretical or artistic representations that privilege opposition and tension. The father must be killed, the mother opposed, society battled. Artistic expressions themselves are most often conceived within this kind of oppositional logic. The *maudits*—the *outsider-provocateurs*—who are rejected are the most valued. And the one thing that stands out about them is their having been *maudit* and rejected. None of them have been good comrades or companions in time. Within this logic, the comrades of the time are the officials, the well adjusted. Should we invoke a different logic, one of maximal adhesion and consent? This idea runs through the intellectual field from the pole of a conservative starting point, claiming a noncontemporaneity for itself, sneering at art that's "fine with meaning nothing," finding its ethical posture only in detesting its own epoch (which denies to the users of such logic any positions of honor, any economic and symbolic privileges), moving toward a different pole, a state of emancipation, chronicling "ages of consensus" and announcing the end of the discord so necessary to politics. Of that first pole, there is nothing more to say, for while its reactionary position defends oppositional logic, political confusion lies in wait. The second pole is much more nuanced, much more subtle, and often it's this pole that allows us to envision what a companion in time might be.

The best formulation of this kind of companionship is the kind I've found in a text by Emmanuelle Pireyre. Entitled "Fictions documentaires," her *ars poetica* touches upon the principal issues of our present essay. At first, one might think that in terms of position, nothing would more fully distinguish her posture from oppositional logic. But on the contrary, Emmanuelle Pireyre constantly uses the vocabulary of *cum-*, of rapport, of relation. She posits that "there is a close rapport between the type of literature produced in a particular epoch and its historical and social context, such as the manner in which texts choose their place of origin, the ground upon which they stand." She goes on to multiply terms related to companionship: coincide, accompany . . . To explain it best, we can look at the first example she gives:

If we must choose a distinctive trait of our experience of the real, whether close to us or far away, we may begin by noting the high ratio of time we spend mediating reality through a screen, be it a computer screen or a television screen. We live in an intensive manner in the *company* of our little screens, and these screens disperse—in our living rooms, bedrooms, and offices—a great deal of fact and/or gibberish concerning the world; but for all that, we are neither stupefied nor overwhelmed by our TV or computer screens: rather, we allot them only a certain limited amount of our attention. And this is the second distinctive trait. Our screens are not like cinema screens; in front of a small or medium-sized screen for which we are, in some respects, the projectionist, we rarely forget ourselves, talking out loud about what we see, changing the DVD, clicking on some button, fixing a sandwich, answering the telephone.[9]

This position is contemporary in the third sense of the word. It maintains a "commerce" (Pireyre uses this word ironically) with the time, committing neither to the logic of withdrawal nor to that of opposition, so dear to modernist theorists:

Within this commerce we maintain with our screen companions, it is almost as if every sentence they speak about the world must be distrusted. On the one hand, the world makes such a loud noise, and makes it so well that it pours ideas down into us like a rainstorm, but on the other hand these thousands of ideas are not given to us in a pure, accessible state, but rather as if packaged; and unwrapping them constitutes a good part of our practices and manners of writing.[10]

The logic of *cum-* is deployed throughout here, as Pireyre adopts a posture, a singularity that is no longer "in relation to or in opposition to the social group" but rather one that twists, plays with, and juxtaposes languages especially, seeking out dissonance: in short, it finds a mode of being in equivocation.

Equivocation, then, as another name for this companionship

with time: for, it's worth repeating, renouncing opposition in no way signifies consent or blissful acceptance. We read here a manifesto of the *cum-*, a survival manual for the companionship that abstracts itself from oppositional logic. To be with the times, to be a comrade of the times, is to slip into its hidden folds, to occupy it, inhabit it, to reconfigure it and make it visible. The conclusion that Emmanuelle Pireyre draws is perfectly clear, as she posits a "redeployment toward the plural":

> If the relationship with the world is not an open antagonism between the I and external reality, but rather a slipping, a movement of the I into and out of phenomena and social discourse, with the desire of tracing the paths of these phenomena, reconfiguring them, rendering them habitable—in that case our attention is turned toward plurality, toward social constructions, extensions of the We with variable dimensions.[11]

This idea is hardly an isolated one. Let's turn from French literature to a great international success. Roberto Saviano argues for a similar position, relatively speaking, particularly in a passage in *Gomorrah* where he brings together the naturalist novelist Luciano Bianciardi and Pier Paolo Pasolini.[12] No more writer as terrorist, and no more writer as pirate: from now on, we have the *embedded*[13] writer, in the sense of being immersed in the real, about which there is no preexisting discourse available, only the proofs that the writer brings together and renders visible. One could readily multiply examples of this from literature and artistic practice, examples that would serve to illustrate the practice of *mise en contexte,*[14] the putting together and the creation of context out of the prose of the world and its hidden realities.

In this practice, there is something of "compositionism" (another word formed with the *cum-* prefix) associated with Bruno Latour, who wrote its manifesto.[15] Compositionism is distinguished, first, from oppositional logic (as the name implies), and second, it formulates a very rare proposition concerning modernity and the modern (as Jauss understands them). It is thus of considerable interest to this work. However, Latour plays with the very signs of modernism in his compositionist manifesto, distorting its most emblematic genre, the manifesto, and mimicking the most celebrated of them all, the *Communist Manifesto*.

But it is surely less the word *manifesto* that should interest us in our inquiry into the contemporary (though, to be sure, to render something manifest is to render it present), and much more the word *compositionist,* especially in the first sense Latour gives it, as a path outside of or above critique—which, in my view, echoes the problematization of oppositional logic maintained in the word *contemporary.* As this touches upon delicate matters (a critique of critique?), it is important not to caricature his thought. It's not a matter of a critique of critique but rather a new use of critique. The world of critique rests upon the essential idea that there is a division and even an opposition between the world of reality and the world of appearances. Critique helps us break through the wall of appearances, beyond which we find the *real* world. For Bruno Latour, there is no beyond, and there is no fundamental division between reality and appearances, just as there is no longer one between the human and the nonhuman. Compositionist logic suspends the critical gesture of division and distancing and instead favors a constructivist approach. And here we discover some formulations quite similar to those of Emmanuelle Pireyre, such as when Latour expresses the following wish:

> We need to have a much more material, much more mundane, much more immanent, much more realistic, much more embodied definition of the material world if we wish to compose a common world.[16]

This is a good instance of our third semantization of *contemporary.* Composing a common world requires a certain companionship in time. Companionship in time composes the common world.

We can begin to see a logic emerging. From the modal under-standing of *contemporary* to what it is that *contemporary* might mean, the power of the prefix *cum-* makes itself felt: with, together, not separated, *inséparé*.[17] With the time, with the times, the times together. Thus the concept of history that the contemporary works with contests modern history, founded as it is upon a separation, a sequentiality, a succession.

THE NONMODERN CONTEMPORARY

So this is a more serious subject than some might think. The con-temporary is not just some ultramodern sequence, not the most recent modern, not the ultimate actualization of the modern, as soothing as that thought might be to some. It's another mode of being in time, in history, in the world. And in saying this, I'm only extending certain ideas that Bruno Latour expressed twenty years ago.[18] Maybe all that was missing was the word *contemporary*. The substantivation of the word came after his essay was published, and it lends a new currency to his work.

We might first recall his principal ideas to see how they fit with the theory of the contemporary that is now gradually emerging. For some years now, the representation of the world and of time has been undergoing modification, in the sense of beginning to contest the modern representation (Bruno Latour found the dra-matic epochal moment in the symptomatic, but only symptomatic, year 1989, that "miraculous" year, not only because of the fall of the Berlin Wall but also because that year saw the "first confer-ences on the condition of the planet as a whole"). But unlike other thinkers, Latour did not postulate an antimodern or a postmodern condition of any kind (both of those terms being too caught up in the schemas of modern thought, as I will show later); instead, he called modernity an illusion that was in the process of being unmasked. An illusion, a belief that was largely imposed but in fact was never anything but a belief—which explains his title: *We Have Never Been Modern*.

Now, this rejection of belief in the modern corresponds generally to the meaning of the word *contemporary* in the sense I have been trying to explore. In fact, for Latour, modernity is above all a singular conception concerning time; modernity is a time that passes and never returns:

> Modernity comes in as many versions as there are thinkers or journalists, yet all its definitions point, in one way or another, to the passage of time. The adjective "modern" designates a new regime, an acceleration, a rupture, a revolution in time.[19]

Modernity is that fissure, that separation, that conception of the world founded on distinction. In this sense, Latour seconds Jauss before parting company with him. Jauss's text never ceases to invest in the vocabulary of the irreversible passage of time, of the frontier, of separation, all of which are at work in the word *modern*:

> The word *modern* marks the dividing line between today and yesterday, between what, at a given moment, counts as new and what counts as old. To be more precise, and to put the point in terms of fashion, a most instructive phenomenon in this regard, *modern* marks the dividing line between that which is newly produced and that which the newly produced has sidelined, between what was still in yesterday and what is already out today.[20]

Here Jauss evokes a vision of modernity that arises from the European nineteenth century, but he notes that this sense of the word reflects an "experience of time" that consists of "eliminating the past." (For his part, Latour notes this "bizarre" quality of the modern, the idea of a time that passes irreversibly annulling everything behind it.) This modern idea of time is "original" in a sense, insofar as it is precisely what motivates the usage of the word at the beginning of the Christian era:

> In the earliest sources, the word has nothing more than a technical meaning; it marks the *boundaries* of the current, which is what one might expect from its etymological origins.[21]

Here is the nub of the issue: the word *modern* implies a representation of time based on the idea of a boundary. And this is what we've inherited. In the same way, we've inherited an awareness of having been "separated from the past by a new era,"[22] which signifies more deeply that we have inherited a conception of time as a sequence of eras. Leaving one, entering another, leaving, entering . . . So time appears like a succession of stations on an irreversible forward journey. Modernity—whether we call it modern times, the age of Enlightenment, or the age of modernity—radicalizes this concept, turning it into an exclusive ideology (though this is not a point Jauss makes). It radicalizes the concept in the sense that it creates a linearity, where before, *antiquitas* and *modernitas* could coexist on a continuum, the first forming the horizon of the second, bringing it back to life, resubstantiating it. The awareness of opposition, distinction, separation, that arose was soon so powerful that the period that chose modernity as its coat of arms, the European nineteenth century, injected it into itself. It was no longer a matter of being different from the ancients but of the period defining itself by "always separating itself from itself"[23]—that is, it defines itself as essentially opposition. More important is "the changed historical self-understanding that manifests itself in this modernity,"[24] an essentially separated identity. As Latour says,

> time's arrow is unambiguous: one can go forward, but then one must break with the past; one can choose to go backward, but then one has to break with the modernizing avant-gardes, which have broken radically with their own past.[25]

Up to this point, Jauss would probably agree. But perhaps less so with what follows:

> This diktat organized modern thought until the last few years—without, of course, having any effect on the practice of mediation, a practice that has always mixed up epochs, genres, and ideas as heterogeneous as those of the premoderns.[26]

Modernity as a diktat: it's a powerful image. We might prefer to think of it as a matter of two differing imaginaries, one in the form of an arrow, the other in the form of a whirlpool. The first is modern, the second, according to Latour, premodern; I would add that it's also contemporary. But I'm not at all saying that the contemporary is a return to the premodern. Instead, we must understand the contemporary as a pausing, a suspension of the representation of time as an arrow. It renews contact with what time is: heterogeneous, mixed, a collection of subjectivities and collectivities. In this regard, the contemporary is, as Latour would say, very "non-modern (or amoderm)"[27] and not postmodern, because the prefix *post-* does not renounce the imaginary of the arrow.

Contrary to what is often said, the word *contemporary* reveals an unsuspected power, precision, accuracy. It seizes the problem of historical identity exactly where the problem is posed, at the level of the imaginary. To the imaginary of separation, it proposes an imaginary of confraternity, of coexistence, but the more it renews contact with other, nonmodern imaginaries, it does not erase the "diktat" of the modern that it carries within itself. Superimpositions (*cum-*), not substitutions.

But what has happened to make modern temporality appear as simply one possibility among others? Or for temporality to be conceived no longer as a given but as an elaboration, as a variant? Or for all temporalities to become co-temporalities, contemporaries? What this inquiry will reveal, again, corresponds rather well to the ideas that Latour advanced. The modern schema of self-representation was a minority one, but it has been largely hegemonic. Henceforth it becomes submerged under "crowds of humans, and non-human environments"—it cracks; it can no longer hold. It appears like an incongruity in the face of the non-modern majority. "It was the systematic connection of entities in a coherent whole that constituted the flow of modern time."[28] But henceforth this flow is turbulent, opened up to the whirlpool, to brouhaha.

PRINCIPLES OF THE STUDY

This essay is consecrated to these whirlpools, these turbulences, and it postulates that brouhaha provides the philosophic, aesthetic, and political meaning of the contemporary, whether considered from a perspective that is epochal (i.e., as our epoch), modal (as a mode of being in historical time), or notional (disciplinary and institutional). So long restrained, the brouhaha will emerge as a historical marker of our time and as a mode for rereading history. If our contemporary moment is a distinct one, it is not only because it is characterized by brouhaha but even more because this has always characterized the present, the very definition of which is a field of uninterrupted controversies. But it's not just any brouhaha. Within epochs, it's not the same people who speak, in the same places, on the same subjects, for the same stakes. These variations are critical to historical differences, which arise out of a reconfiguration of public spheres. To participate in the elaboration of the present is a privilege that has evolved with the times.

Acknowledging this poses a difficulty for the essayist who wants to talk about it. How to account for the brouhaha without either restraining it or allowing it to overwhelm us? For, if a too orderly account would be suspect, it seems impossible to approach this multiplicity head-on and even more impossible to make it visible, to make it perceived and understood. Its multiplicity demands a strategy and a point of entry. So, I began my inquiry within this third period in the history of the word *contemporary,* which has been transformed into a substantive for some ten years now, thanks especially to the proliferation of the question, What is the contemporary? A question that has traversed the globe, giving rise to a vast movement of critical inquiry. All evidence (the repetition and concentration in a given period) suggests a set or a series. But a series characterized by its difference or its diversity. So we can interrogate it on these principles. By asking, in particular, who, over these last ten years, has been posing this question, and in what areas—territorial, disciplinary, professional, political—they operate, and what epistemological and discursive regimes they deploy.

This is our point of entry, which will function as the thread of our inquiry, almost its scenario, allowing us to navigate from Rosario to Stanford, from a provincial center of contemporary art to one of the centers of the academic world, since, thanks to the archival powers that new technologies offer us and the ability to type into any available search engine that simple question— "*¿Qué es lo contemporáneo?*"—*Zum,* a local fanzine, finds itself at the origin of an almost global inquiry, one that will lead us to Argentina, to Italy, to France, to Germany, to the United States, to China, to Chile, to India, to Hong Kong, and to many other places besides. And because of this technology, some random student studying communications, some random artist or thinker living out in the middle of nowhere, will immediately find himself or herself in dialogue with Giorgio Agamben, Nancy Fraser, Donna Haraway, the collective known as Raqs Media, Brian O'Doherty, Chika Okeke-Agulu, Manuel De Landa, Gayatri Chakravorty Spivak, Cuauhtémoc Medina, Philippe Vasset, or Stuart Hall. These last few sentences form both a thesis and a method. The thesis is as follows: never before has an interrogation into historical identity been so widely shared and so profoundly globalized. And that also means that never have potential and actual controversies been so intense and so political. The method is as follows: to do justice to the thesis, we will (virtually) survey the world and we will listen. We will listen to a multitude of actors, classifying and sorting as little as possible, not effacing them or their presence. This will not be a matter of name dropping but rather of a choral inquiry in which no one is reduced to an extra. We will try to reveal and make heard the world of the contemporary, or rather the worlds of the contemporary, as they are constituted in places, words, and actions that are often conflictual. We are all more accustomed to an inverse method of inquiry—the kind that would take, for example, Giorgio Agamben's essay[29] as the definitive word on the subject, both retrospective and prophetic, and then go on to analyze every phenomenon of the contemporary from that point of view. Our inquiry will be quite different—for while it will certainly take Agamben's book into account, we will situate it within a series, observing the conditions of possibility and of actual existence within a larger milieu. From that milieu will emerge the principal characteristics of the contemporary: indistinction, unseparateness, co-temporality, the pluralization of public spaces, dehierarchization, and so on. This isn't about constructing a narrative of the contemporary, tempting us to unify something that can't be unified around a fictional central point; rather, it's about documenting narratives and histories and constructing an archive. The goal is to think and write about the contemporary without reproducing the hermeneutic modes (linearity, succession, sequentiality) that the contemporary has put into crisis.

Each series therefore begins with an occurrence of the question, What is the contemporary? that opens up one of the essential stations or resting stops along the way for us in thinking about our representations, and especially our cultural representations: exhibitions, the media, literature and publishing, controversies concerning art and culture, the role of the institutions, history, and archaeology. One might object that there's no longer any real reason to devote an essay to the contemporary as expressed in representations, artistic practices, and cultural forms in a world that no longer recognizes distinctions like nature–culture, humans–nonhumans. Fine. But we must remember that it's precisely in the field of representations that the modern hypothesis is strongest, that the consciousness of a collective temporality based on sequentiality and succession has installed itself. This is the place where resistances and energies most intensely confront another conception of collective time. And it is precisely here, at this place, where I want to situate my work.

Exposition

HORIZONTALITY: ROSARIO, 2004

A few years ago, I was asked to participate in a conference titled "What Is the Contemporary?" This event would be repeated twice more. While I had already organized a conference around this question myself, and I had also edited a volume with the same title—at a moment when Giorgio Agamben's book *What Is an Apparatus?* (containing the short essay on the question of the contemporary) was gaining worldwide success—I saw this series of asking the same question without ever coming up with an answer to be in itself a way of understanding the contemporary.

On one hand, the series marked the end of the process of substantivation—that is, of the word becoming a noun. *Contemporary* is no longer a simple adjective for modifying subjects, objects, or an epoch, an adjective long derided for its emptiness and inconsistency; now it's a substantive, whose exact substance is precisely what we're questioning. With the intuitive sense that it concerns all of us, collectively.

On the other hand (and perhaps in a contradictory manner), while this series may have marked the end of the substantivation process, that process was nevertheless shown to be, if not impossible to be finished with, at the very least incomplete. Because part

27

of what's so striking is how often we see this same question, this very same formula, signaling the failure of any attempt at a clear and univocal meaning.

So it had to be enough, and this is still the case today, to simply let oneself be carried along with this movement, this interrogation of the historical identity of our time, and to retrace it. Contrary to what one might believe, Giorgio Agamben didn't begin this inquiry into the "contemporary." Instead, the vanguard can be found in two provincial places, Rouen and Rosario, each in the shadow of its respective capital, Paris and Buenos Aires. And the manner in which the question was posed is just as significant as the question itself, for on one hand, the question arose within a center of contemporary art and, on the other, inside a school of architecture.

Why is it so significant that this question arises out of an art center? If we take a step back and analyze how the term *contemporary* became so dominant, we notice that museums have played a major role. Generally speaking, for museums, the shift to the contemporary was less a question of chronology and more about the transformation of the institution itself. Simply put, it was a matter of museums transforming themselves into centers of art— that is, transforming the public space of art; the museum changes from being a sacred space devoted to contemplation into a new, multifunctional space oriented toward experience: an art center.

As we shall see later on in our inquiry, the Centre Pompidou, in the Beaubourg area of Paris, played an important role in this historical shift, including from the very beginning as part of its foundational structure, a research library, an institute for contemporary music, a center for industrial design, a stage for performances, a cinema, and a museum; as such, it constituted a reorganization of territory, with political implications. In short, the museum becoming a center was not the result of the passage from modern to contemporary, for the works within it remained the same; rather, it was the transformation of the museum into a center that effected the transition from modern to contemporary. "Museum of contemporary art" and "center for modern art" are phrases that don't really make much sense, because they presuppose entirely different public spaces for art. But a center for contemporary art can certainly include within it a museum of modern art, as is the case with the Pompidou.

In this sense, the fact that the question was first posed by the Centro de Expresiones Contemporáneas (CEC) seems symbolically important to me, more so than if it had been raised by more spectacular and prominent centers like the Pompidou or LA MoCa (the Los Angeles Museum of Contemporary Art, founded a few years after the Pompidou). In the CEC's name, the word "art" is omitted, and in its place we see that the subject is "expressions," or sometimes "practices." The language the CEC in Rosario uses on its website to describe itself is carefully chosen, insisting on its choice of terminology:

> We take as our guiding principles the three words that form the name of our institution: center, expressions, and contemporary.
>
> Center, meaning a point of convergence, a space of intersection, etc.
>
> Expressions, as synonym for signs, gestures, relational mechanisms, languages, invitations.
>
> Contemporary, as coexistence within time, unity with the century.
>
> The word "expressions" has quickly come to displace the word "art," which limited itself to those things conventionally denoted by the term, leaving aside its possible applications in other domains such as design, architecture, fashion, etc.

The project was first formulated in 1992 and formally inaugurated in 1995, which is surprising considering the neoliberal Peronism dominating Argentina at that time, under President Carlos Menem. The times were marked more by a general withdrawal from the public sphere than by an investment in culture. But Rosario is not Buenos Aires, or rather Rosario is anything but Buenos Aires. What was unimaginable in the capital could become reality in one of its potential rivals, one of those cities that tried to compete by proposing a countercultural model. The CEC, then, is a municipal rehabilitation project, involving harbor-side warehouses on the Paraná River, a project called the "Paseo de las Artes y el río Paraná." But the primary goal was not to create a museum of contemporary art, which the city would later create in 2004 with the Museo de Arte Contemporáneo de Rosario (MACRo), an annex to the Museo Municipal de Bellas Artes Juan B. Castagnino. At that later time, the city was simply trying to follow the national and regional (i.e., Latin American) trend initiated by the 2001 Museo de Arte Latinamericano de Buenos Aires (MALBA), a movement toward the "museumification" of contemporary art.[1]

However, in 1992, the goal was something altogether different—much more modest in terms of visibility, true, but much more experimental in terms of the public space in question. Besides, the municipality entrusted the idea of the center to artists from multiple disciplines as well as some prominent people from the social world. The first director was representative of the emphasis on various modes of practice. María de los Angeles "Chiqui" González is an attorney, academic, actress, and playwright who specializes in creating and transmitting material for young audiences. She is also a great example of the idea that a career in "civil service" is often a stepping-stone toward a political career, because in 2007, Chiqui González was named minister of innovation and culture in the province of Santa Fe.

The question, What is the contemporary? arose not out of the creation of the center but later on, in 2004, that is, in the same year as the inauguration of MACRo, as if the creation of a museum of contemporary art posed a problem to the Center for Contemporary Expressions in the same city, such that they needed to reflect about this shared idea. This hypothesis is purely theoretical, I must admit, or let's say it seems plausible, because my sources on this are minimal. Without the archival resources of the Internet, I would never have come across the CEC or its magazine, *Zum*, which was barely more than a fanzine, and I would never have been able to put together the genealogy I am exploring. The magazine is described on the CEC website in the following way: "*Zum* is a publication of the CEC, edited and conceived by students in design, journalism, and communication." We also read, "The magazine *Zum* is a publication of the CEC edited and created by the young people in our city."

"Young people in our city" and "students" are not quite the same thing, but they spring from the same idea. The point is to place a certain notion of authority under suspicion. It's important, then, to underline that the archaeology of this substantivation we're tracing includes, very near its beginning, a "deauthorization" of the word. Without knowing it, the authorities who followed, and symbolically the authority Giorgio Agamben, were joining a movement that was established by actors who were not claiming much authority themselves. The journal presents itself simply as "a site for interaction among students" who can exhibit their work there, a "medium in which all cultural expressions can be made manifest, interact, dialogue, and mingle."

In every issue, the journal prints a heading: "What is the contemporary?" Its recurrence practically becomes its identity. Because of its very modesty, inviting both fragmentary responses and multiple ones, the question we're pursuing receives no definitive answers. But what's important here is something else. What we see developing is, instead, an apparatus that exemplifies the new public space of contemporary art: something much more horizontal, more democratic, more social, more popular. And in fact, the first response that was given to the question (and we must insist that it is truly the first time that the contemporary is explicitly conceptualized) is no different. The contemporary is described as "a way of seeing," a cultural practice denouncing the "culture of elites," an "encounter with mass society and its production." The response also emphasizes the remixing and intermixing of culture between methods and formats, artistic languages and multimedia. It concludes with the essential point: the contemporary is "a process of the democratization of culture."

On this point, the contributors from Rosario are right, because the contemporary epoch, as well as the contemporary as concept, can be seen as opening up access to the realms of social distinction, including the realms of culture. The centers of contemporary art, from the most modest to the most spectacular, are the embodiment of this idea. But, as it so happens, the most modest are the most spectacular. At Rosario, a whole population was called to respond to the question: first and foremost students, but also artists, writers, professors, anthropologists, psychoanalysts, directors of institutions, guitarists, social workers ... An entire population, but not truly *the* entire population, because there's a kind of homogeneity among this group of people: militant and creative, militant for a democratized culture and against the "culture of the elites." As these partial responses, these regimes of speech, accumulate, the impression created becomes cacophonous—democratic certainly, but also cacophonous. And so it was that, with little fanfare, and within a relatively peripheral setting like the Centro de Expresiones Contemporáneas, in Rosario, in Argentina—but perhaps precisely because of its very peripheral nature, so emblematic of the topic in question—the various reflections concerning the contemporary began to develop a number of the traits that would come to characterize it over the next several years. Thinking was shaped into a nondisciplined brouhaha; this way of thinking precedes the so-called representative figures of intellectual authority, who are then tempted to put it into some kind of order, and whose attempts therefore are treated with suspicion. This Rosario moment is inscribed in, and reflects on, the new public space for contemporary expressions: a space that would be more horizontal, more democratic, more social, more popular. Of course, this doesn't mean that unexpected distinctions can't come to the fore, and it would be a mistake to imagine that this space of discussion and reflective analysis never excluded anything. Nonetheless, a different "order of discourse" emerges, emblematic for a number of reasons: as I said, the first theoretical reflection of the contemporary comes to us from an old province in a region otherwise considered to be peripheral (Rosario, Argentina). It's a reaction to the institutionalization of contemporary Art (with a capital A)—represented by the creation of a museum for contemporary art in the town—and this reaction comes from those who clearly want to substitute expressions for more clearly delineated conceptions of art. This reaction creates a gap between the museum and the contemporary, in terms of public spaces. The centers and the museums are not devoted to the same thing; the reactions of the magazine contributors in Rosario indicate a point that we'll encounter again later: there can indeed be a kind of conflict between the institutional and the contemporary, and the contemporary can become a site of conflict between those who primarily value creating it and those who want to institutionalize it.

THE INSTITUTION OF THE MUSEUM

However, there is also a history of the contemporary in museums. Or rather, two histories.

Let us now leave Rosario in order to recall that, unlike other institutions—the university, for example—the museum, since its very origins, has always provided a place for contemporary works. In the twentieth century, to some extent, museums of modern art have provided this place, but they also tend to share in the old logic of what was called living art, elaborated around the beginning of the nineteenth century. Thus, for example, it was scarcely twenty-five years after the founding of the Louvre museum that a museum for living artists was established in the Palais du Luxembourg—significantly, or at any rate curiously, under the restoration of the monarchy (1814–30).[2] The emphasis on "living artists" soon raised a problem, for it implied that as soon as an artist died, his or her work would be taken down. Such artists faced a period of purgatory since, in the best of circumstances, ten years would have to pass before their works could be displayed at the Louvre. Without a strong heritage mission like the museums devoted to art of the past, and without trying to establish a canon, as would be the case with the creation of museums of modern art, institutions devoted to such art instead made the expression of national spirit their raison d'être, in part conforming to the spirit of the times in Europe, the United States, Russia, and Latin America. They devoted themselves to promoting art that could be called national, in the sense that the word *national* expressed in the nineteenth century. Moreover, these museums did not carry over any of the museographic traditions of the Louvre concerning heritage art.

Nor were those traditions maintained by the first museum to use "contemporary" in its title: the Musée des Écoles étrangères contemporaines was installed in the Jeu de Paume in 1932 and all but openly proclaimed that its goal was to reinforce the image of Paris as the international capital of living art, at the very moment when the Museum of Modern Art (MoMA) in New York was at the dawn of its supremacy. The first instance of the use of the term "contemporary art" in an institution's title came a little later, in 1948, with the foundation of the Institute of Contemporary Art in Boston. This is far more significant, for along with it came a programmatic document that gave rise to a widespread debate in the United States, concerning both ideas and the terms being used; somewhat surprisingly, the debate spilled over into the popular press. Originally called the Boston Museum of Modern Art in 1935, as if it were just an annex of MoMA, the museum freed itself in 1939 by opting first for the title Institute of Modern Art, and then for Institute of Contemporary Art. The transformation from a "museum" to an "institute" is at the very least just as important as that from "modern" to "contemporary." Perhaps the first change can be said to presuppose the second. It was a mutation that later on would have far-reaching effects. "Institute" in Boston had an academic air about it, and the museum declared that it would strive to be a place for panoramic study rather than the site of a coherent collection. But it was clearly the transformation from "modern" to "contemporary" that spilled the most ink, especially because it was accompanied by a manifesto ("'Modern Art' and the American Public"), signed by the director, James S. Plaut, and the president of its governing board, Nelson W. Aldrich.[3] This document was widely shared in institutions and reprinted by the press, and its effects were far more intense than its authors could have ever imagined. Beginning with the title, the reader sees that the goal is to confront the relationship between the American public and modern art; essentially, that implies European art, even more specifically Parisian art, so important to MoMA. The manifesto declares that after the First World War, "modern art failed to speak clearly" and that it has created "a general cult of bewilderment," which in turn has cut off all communication between artist and public.

The manifesto goes further, proclaiming that modern art had become "dated and academic," and it listed some guiding principles: if the artist wished to remain ahead of his or her time, there must be a reduction in the gap between the artist and public and, consequently, a reduction in the need for interpretation; an institution collecting contemporary art must have as its principal mission the activity of selecting artworks according to artistic principles, principles that of course include excellence, but an excellence that the contemporary public (and not some hypothetical future public) can comprehend. The manifesto continues: since the public for art is always growing, artists must accept the role of "spiritual leadership," inspired by human nature; the art of the present day cannot continue to be judged solely by the standards of an intellectual revolution from the early twentieth century, which came to an end with the Second World War, but at the same time art cannot be simply a form of reaction or conservatism. In the view of its founders, the Institute for Contemporary Art must be at once a place of exhibition, a site for publication, and a forum for the integration of art with commerce and industry. These principles called for a name change:

> In order to give full emphasis to these objectives, and in order to disassociate the policy and program of this institution from the widespread and injurious misunderstandings which surround the term "modern art," the Corporation has today changed its name from The Institute of Modern Art to The Institute of Contemporary Art.

The text exploded like a bomb in the East Coast art world (at that time the most powerful in the world), largely dominated by MoMA. And all the more so for the way it could later be connected with the exploitation of artistic disputes during the Cold War.[4] The riposte came from MoMA, which, with the support of the Whitney Museum of American Art, persuaded a group of "dissident" art directors from the ICA to sign a text of conciliation (or perhaps of capitulation) titled "A Statement of Modern Art."[5] Presenting these institutions as being devoted, above all else, to the art of their time, the signatories (including Alfred H. Barr, the highly influential director of MoMA) wanted to clarify their stance on recent controversies concerning modern art. As it turned out, the ICA made no converts, and it had only a marginal influence on the new sites devoted to contemporary art. Nonetheless, it opened up a museum-based critique of modern art, that is, a critique of its public space (which was, at basis, a critique of MoMA, which is just as much an ideology as a museum). This critique comes to life in our second story.

In a way, this became the second moment of the encounter between the museum as institution and the contemporary: a moment that saw the birth of the Centre Pompidou and the New Museum of Contemporary Art in New York, both having been conceived, if not in downright opposition to MoMA, then at least with the hope of creating a new paradigm for the public space of contemporary art, the two initiatives taking place almost simultaneously. At the Centre Pompidou, the principal innovation consisted in bringing together what would come to be called a *cluster*, a center that grouped various entities together: a public library, a center for commercial and industrial creativity, an institute for research and for musical/acoustical coordination, and the national museum of modern art. The most powerfully expressed idea concerned the multidisciplinary and the interdisciplinary aspect of contemporary creativity conceived as a whole, a whole that *also* integrated contemporary art. This is an element of primary importance, a rupture with what is called the Greenbergian vision of art,[6] which was also the vision of MoMA. Apart from this interdisciplinarity, the nature of the public space imagined here breaks also with the famous "white cube" ideology.[7] The visitor's first experience of the Centre Pompidou is an experience of space: the space connecting the plaza and the forum and the space that, thanks to the escalators, leads up to an extraordinary view of the city. The first design imagined for the museum was also going to be something of a rupture, because it involved privileging the modularity of exhibition spaces and foregrounding the museum's public space, offering for the museum-goer the sensation of a random stroll through the cityscape inside the museum itself, in the style of Baudelaire's flâneur, Benjamin's arcades, and Debord's situationists. While that design was abandoned in favor of a second, much more traditional one, it nonetheless influenced many other art centers that rejected the "white cube" in favor of a more personalized, erratic space. Another very important element of the Centre Pompidou design was its intention of revitalizing a city neighborhood in decline, and in this it succeeded admirably, transforming the area into one of the most expensive in Paris. From then on, practically all centers of contemporary art incorporated the idea of urban revitalization. At the same time, in 1977, the New Museum of Contemporary Art was founded in New York as a distinct contemporary alternative to MoMA, not only because the art exhibited there was more recent but also because the New Museum saw itself as a place that would bring together initiatives from a number of experimental centers; because it had almost no permanent collection; and finally, because this new kind of space was presented specifically as a site for debate concerning what was current and not at all a space for the exhibition of artifacts. Once again, experience and interdisciplinarity, debate and brouhaha, were favored over aesthetic contemplation.

These two models, among others, opened up a new era in the relationship between publics and contemporary creativity, and they were triumphant in a way that is quite impossible today to quantify or map,[8] given the growth in the establishment of centers of art and creativity that have been based on similar principles: the experience of a multifunctional and interdisciplinary space, a project with local political impact, all within the public sphere in the strict sense of that phrase as a site for debate. Among these innumerable centers, one notes the Centro de Expresiones Contempóraneas of Rosario, where for the first time the question was posed: what is the contemporary? The horizontality we noticed there, and the transformation of publics and of spaces, are also manifest spectacularly in the Centre Pompidou and elsewhere.

EXHIBITION IDEOLOGIES

Exhibition spaces constitute, at least at first, a node for understanding the contemporary. Owing to their proliferation across the planet, exhibition spaces have become the model for one of the most globalized ways of structuring space, one that has influenced a great variety of issues and subjects. Regardless of what we might wish, or what we might say. For many, "contemporary" is first and foremost a word that one encounters within an exhibition space. And from that encounter emerges the most common understanding of the term, and as a result the term's default definition. The center for contemporary art is therefore one of the privileged worlds of the contemporary, one that helps shape its meaning.

Yet every public space, and especially any public exhibition space, carries with it an idea, a history, perhaps even an ideology. These two stories involving the contemporary and the museum—in Boston and in Beaubourg—tell us quite clearly that the center for contemporary art emerged in opposition to the museum of modern art. But what exactly was the center opposed to? There is a fundamental link between several ideas that the word *contemporary* throws into question. The givens are museum, art, modern. When thought conjointly, they spill beyond the borders of art itself and touch upon the topics of space and time, and upon how we live within them. As the artist-theoretician Brian O'Doherty puts it, "if art has any cultural reference (apart from being 'culture'), surely it is in the definition of our space and time."[9] Contrary to what some have said, it could be argued that the only museum that exists is the museum of modern art, or rather that every museum is a museum of modern art—that is, keeping in mind the conjunction of those three terms. *Artification*—transforming artifacts into objects of art—and *museumification* imply each other in the modern *epistēmē*. As soon as we evoke the idea of the museum, we commit to a mode of organizing the perceptible world in a specifically modern way. And when one is conscious of this profound linkage among objects, sites, forms of reception and of exhibition, the category of the aesthetic but also our perceiving and making sense of the perceptible world—at that point, using new terms like "center" or "contemporary" is clearly not a trivial matter.

Every museum is a museum of modern art. It's perhaps a bit excessive to state it in these terms; let's try to be more specific. Though the story is well known, even legendary, it's worth recalling the key episodes. The origin of the story dates from the Belvedere garden of Pope Julius II (toward the beginning of the sixteenth century), when, after having a statue of *Laocöon* brought to him, the pope began to assemble a collection of objects separated from their actual, generally religious use, and now, following their displacement from that use, he gave them a new function: an aesthetic function. "And suddenly a whole other conception of the world emerged from within Christianity," as it was stated during a recent lecture given by "Walter Benjamin," conducted by a series of actors and actresses throughout the world.[10] The lecture was more than likely written by Goran Djordjevic, a conceptual artist who is the creator of the strange Museum of American Art in Berlin, to whom we owe the *Recent Writings* of the aforementioned Walter Benjamin.[11] Despite its fictional elements, this lecture, half-serious and half-playful, has had considerable influence on what is to follow. I encountered it at the art center Le Plateau in Paris, as part of the exhibition titled *Les fleurs américaines*.

He made the point that any religious painting will no longer provoke a genuflection when repurposed for aesthetic contemplation. But when returned to the originally intended location, generally a church, the painting then reintegrates itself into a religious setting and mode of being. This is why history tells us, quite correctly, that the era we call modernity began in that Belvedere garden, that an unprecedented occupation of space and time came into being, and that an extraordinary fate for objects was invented. One expression sums it up perfectly: museum of modern art. The Belvedere garden is the first museum of modern art (remembering that there are no museums except museums of modern art, no matter what objects are displayed there). The presentation of objects as art objects within a sanctified space, abstracting them from their other usages to bring them together under the category of art—this is precisely what creates modernity. The museum as institution, as imaginary, as structure, constitutes art, which itself can only be modern: just as the center constitutes contemporary art (though the word *art* surely no longer fits, remaining like an anachronism, or as a kind of reflex[12]), as we have seen and will see again. The center makes contemporary art indeterminable, tentacular—which is a fairly good description of the worlds of the contemporary. The artifacts themselves matter little. The museum transforms artifacts (statues of gods and paintings of icons) into art objects. Thus, the conference speaker tells us, "only those artifacts created after the appearance of museums can be considered as real works of art." We see how impossible it would be to write a history of art that only discussed the artifacts themselves. This is systematically the case. Even the best thought-out theories, even the most convincing studies, fail if they only focus on the objects of art.

But the story of the invention of museums produced a new history of art. Telling its story retrospectively, it detemporalizes art in order to integrate it into its own scheme. It places the museum narrative within history; the conference speaker goes so far as to say that it is a matter of "colonizing" history: "the museums which are the incarnation of the history of art have become the instruments of that colonization of history by the history of art." In fact, museums become less museums of art and more specifically art history museums (insofar as they exhibit a history); the role these museums play in teaching the values proper to modern history is by no means trivial. Little by little, the narrative of art history, concretized in the museums, has developed a number of characteristics that the broader field of history uses to organize its subject matter: chronologies, with sequences and successions; a decisive accent on the national organization (from the early nineteenth century on); the notions of the author and the original. This apparatus is readily visible in the work that gives the key to the program: Giorgio Vasari's *Lives of the Most Eminent Painters, Sculptors, and Architects* is considered a foundational text in the history of art, foundational precisely because it establishes art as a reality both modern and capable of colonizing history. We should note as well that Vasari was establishing an art that for him was contemporary. For the museum narrative makes no distinction between works of the past and works of the present, as requiring any particular, differing kind of treatment. As proof of this, the world's fairs of the nineteenth century, which were the first exhibitions of the contemporary art of their time, were thought of using exactly the same logic, notably with the appearance of national pavilions.

Museums are often compared to religious buildings. There's good reason for this. For one thing, it's important to remember, the objects that the first museums converted into art objects were often taken from religious buildings. For another, the museums as churches have the exorbitant power of converting their objects into a reality that transcends them. Moreover, there are very few examples in human history of public spaces that are used neither for production nor for consumption. The museum is a kind of space clearly defined and delimited—that is to say, a closed space—in which the magic (in the sense of magical thinking) of the religious or the aesthetic sentiment can take place. Museums and religious buildings are comparable, too, in being sometimes accompanied by libraries, although the study that takes place in a library confers a utilitarian quality that the two buildings otherwise lack. Museums and religious buildings share the same destiny, at least in certain parts of the world. And already we see people visiting the museums like witnesses to the history of museums, in the same way they visit churches without any particular religious sentiment.[13]

So what exactly was it that brought the museums of modern art (a phrase we now see as tautological) into crisis? What is it that has changed in our relation to those spaces such that, at least in certain regions of the world (the Western bourgeois world), it has led us to experience museum spaces as desacralized, from now on devoid of the sacred, in a similar manner as our rapport with religious buildings? There is an internal answer to the question in Brian O'Doherty's book *Inside the White Cube* (and in the preface to the French edition by the art historian Patricia Falguières):

> The history of modernism is intimately framed by that space [that is, the gallery]; or rather, the history of modern art can be correlated with changes in that space and in the way we see it. Today, we have reached a point where it is not the art we see first, but the space (a cliché of the age is to ejaculate over the space on entering a gallery). An image comes to mind of a white space, ideal space, that, more than any single picture, may be the archetypal image of twentieth century art; it clarifies itself through a process of historical inevitability usually attached to the art it contains.
>
> The ideal gallery subtracts from the artwork all cues that interfere with the fact that it is "art." The work is isolated from everything that would detract from its own evaluation of itself. This gives the space a presence possessed by other spaces where conventions are preserved through the repetition of a closed system of values. Some of the sanctity of the church, the formality of the courtroom, the mystique of the experimental laboratory joins with chic design to produce a unique chamber of aesthetics. So powerful our the perceptual fields of force within this chamber that, once outside it, art can lapse into secular status. Conversely, things become art in a space where powerful ideas about art focus on them.[14]

And perhaps O'Doherty puts it best—in this book with so many well-phrased ideas, ideas that are as crucial as they are striking:

> Unshadowed, white, clean, artificial—the space is devoted to the technology of esthetics.[15]

O'Doherty's book opens up a new way of understanding art through its content and contexts. It shows how the history of art (that episode stretching from the sixteenth century to the twentieth century) works itself out in the exhibition space, which is the space of conversion, and which finds its strongest, most concrete form in what the book calls the "white cube," a phrase we will use as well. The white cube's ascendency took some time, only truly coming to the fore in the twentieth century. This new, powerful, and decisive manner led to a way "to correlate the internal history of paintings with the external history of how they were hung."[16] O'Doherty reminds us that "the nineteenth century mind was taxonomic, and the nineteenth century eye recognized hierarchies of genre and the authority of the frame."[17] The twentieth century intensified the hanging wall's purity, conferring the greatest possible "aesthetic essence" to the artifact. This "conversion chamber" influenced artistic production itself in the senses of flatness and objecthood, concepts from the formalist theory that O'Doherty opposes. For him, as Patricia Falguières puts it, "the history of the exhibition space as he traces it was closed, as was the history of modernism."[18] Closed by the actors themselves, by the artists and theorists, including O'Doherty as well, all of whom, under the banner of "institutional critique," have in fact developed a wide-ranging critique of art institutions, their exhibition spaces, their ideology of exhibition, and their construction of values, both symbolic and economic. One constant among all these events—notably during the explosive years from 1965 to 1975—is a questioning of the closed space of exhibition, with its utopic atmosphere in which the "work of art" is kept separate from the triviality of the real world, deriving its character *as* work of art from that very separation. To open up these spaces, profaning the white cube, blurring the distinction between inside and outside, between actor and spectator, aesthetic condition and economic or political condition, object and space, contemplation and action: these are the acts that progressively lead to the collapse of the institution and the expression "museum of modern art." But that collapse goes beyond the exhibition spaces and involves, much more generally, common spaces themselves.

One of the strongest signs of this is the almost endless proliferation of new centers for contemporary art, which testifies to a new relationship with shared experiences. A new relationship because the limits and borderlines are no longer so clear and no longer arise from the monumental approach that would have identified them; on the contrary, their propagation seems to render their borders indeterminate. We can see this phenomenon come to life in works of fiction more vividly than in works of theory. For example, it is present in a vast anti-utopian work by the French writer Philippe Vasset, whose first paragraph reads as follows:

> We had entirely ceased addressing strangers: in our garages, transformed for the evening into a theater or a gallery, there were now only family and friends. But note: if a stranger had arrived for a private viewing or presentation, he would have been warmly welcomed. He would have been invited to participate in the play, to stroll among the works, to help himself to a glass of punch, and even the artist, immediately abandoning his close friends, would have made an effort to ask his opinion, and would have listened, and would have thanked him.[19]

Vasset's text, describing transformations in Western bourgeois lifestyles, presents us with the paradox that, at a time when sites for exhibiting art are proliferating almost to infinity, their specificity as museums of modern art vanishes. The museum apparatus, as a place apart from the profane sphere of experience, as a sacred place of aesthetic contemplation, no longer exists—even in the museums. The insides and the outsides of exhibitions are no longer distinct. We can see this practice brought to its absurd conclusion in the evolution of heritage museums, notably their use of audio guides that are always becoming more technologically perfected, more enhanced, and always more connected. So it's no surprise to see that at the Louvre, you can now enjoy the video game experience thanks to the Nintendo DS that the museum chose for its audio guide; you can inhabit several spaces at the same time.

Absurd, yes, but this fact allows us to return to some of our principal propositions so far. The museum is a project that establishes modern art, and despite its vast development, the project is in ruins—to use the celebrated image of the American art historian Douglas Crimp.[20] The term *contemporary art* denotes less a transformation of artifacts and more a transformation of exhibition, of shared sense experience. There is no essence of contemporary art. There are only conditions.

CONTEMPORARY: BROUHAHA, MULTITUDE

This first series has presented a recurrence, a coherence necessary to the beginning of our investigation. The contemporary is perhaps above all else a question of space and of public spheres. In a sense, this should not surprise us, since to share the same time supposes that we inhabit the same space, whether that space is concrete and material or the more abstract sphere of discussion and communication. We began with a concrete space, the democratic bazaar of Rosario, where the question of historical identity was debated without reliance on traditional authorities. The need to call oneself something new and different makes sense, given the enormous social–historical mutations under way. What accompanies the contemporary are the demographic upheavals that followed the Second World War and the subsequent, no less important social and political upheavals: the appearance of a democratic process, influenced by opening up the system to the masses. The resulting conversation began the debate on the contemporary and made the word into a substantive. And the discussion established itself within a dehierarchization of discourses, reflected in this series by the wide-ranging examples presented from a fanzine to a fictional conference, from a manifesto to one of the most important works of theory of the last thirty years.

Within that framework, we have visited a singular, emblematic public space—the museum, along with places of worship and libraries, is one of the rare instances of institutionalized public space, that is to say, one of those rare public spaces that organizes co-presence, contemporaneity. It carries with it an ideology of community proper to the modernity that distinguishes inside and outside, producers and consumers, the sacred and the profane. It is the most developed of all public spaces, the most diversified, to the point of losing its specificity while at the same time becoming emblematic of what the contemporary might say. The adjective *contemporary* in the phrase *center of contemporary art* signals the end of the institution-project of the museum, the end of a specifically modern form of experience insofar as it is an experience of distinction making. The center for contemporary art is open, without borders. It is in the street, in the city, and it is not a monument, not isolated, not utopian. The contemporary experience of art—which, I must repeat, is essential for understanding the contemporary—is this experience of indistinction, and it is the manifestation of the contemporary *as* indistinction. To inhabit the world no longer means to move from one room to another, from the profane to the sacred, but rather to superimpose the levels of experience upon each other.

At Rosario, again, we discover not a modern community assembling but rather a multitude, in the sense that Michael Hardt and Antonio Negri use the term.[21] And it is with this articulation—modernity–community, contemporary–multitude—that I'll conclude our first series. Of course, Hardt and Negri say little about the idea of the contemporary, preferring to discuss postmodernity. But Negri does raise the topic in an article from 2008,[22] where he notes that he continues to use the term *postmodern* for the potential antagonisms and conflicts it can carry with it. But he says also that the concept of multitude leads inevitably to thinking about contemporaneity. To understand the full scope of the Rosario example, the interpretive model of Hardt and Negri is highly useful. The Centro de Expresiones Contemporáneas is inextricably a site of social, economic, and cultural productions. The collective singularity deployed there is also social, economic, and cultural. So is the new form of capitalism, which our two authors call biopolitical, into which Rosario fits. This "post-Fordist" capitalism is a capitalism of information and networks, one in which the political base is formed not by the masses, not by class, nor by the crowd, but by the multitude. We saw in our investigation of the magazine *Zum* an attempt at collective self-definition that was separate from modern hierarchies and opposed to modern hierarchies. This capacity for self-organization characterizes the multitude, as does its heterogeneity and multiplicity, rendering it impossible to reduce to a unity of the kind that could be expressed by, for example, class or community. The creators and contributors of *Zum* adopt a new logic of struggle, alongside those described by Hardt and Negri, one with consequences both for historical identity and for the use of public spaces, which in turn form that historical identity. In contrast is the weight of the institution of the museum, which tries to unify experience, likewise with social, political, and cultural results. But despite all its struggles, that institution is in ruins.

There is, therefore, a fundamental link between contemporary, brouhaha, and multitude.[23] And once again, this link arises from indistinction, nonseparation.

Media

TECHNOLOGY OF THE IMAGINATION: ROUEN, 2004

At Rosario, we encountered a space and a form of gathering together that were specific to the contemporary. Now we must shift our inquiry and continue somewhere else, but following the same principles. We'll pick up the thread of the global debate over the contemporary, working inductively toward our goal, avoiding the certitudes that previous studies offer and being attentive to the form of our inquiry. We will listen to what is being said and try to pluck out one or two key ideas in order to—eventually and patiently—make our way to a coherent conception of the contemporary.

As was the case with our first inquiry in Rosario, our second series leads off the beaten path, for we will be focusing our attention on a publication from an institution that is not considered to be an elite academic institution: the École nationale supérieure d'architecture de Normandie, or ENSAN.[1] It's as if it were first necessary for the word *contemporary* to become a substantive on the periphery. But before we turn our attention to this publication, a couple of comments need to be made. First, the example of museums has shown how much our ideas of public spaces (both spaces and spheres) structure our approach to the contemporary, especially in its relation to the modern. Second, we must recall just how central to postmodernity architectural theory and expressions have been. Perry Anderson says that architecture was the art that introduced the term *postmodernity* into public discourse. Books by Robert Venturi (*Learning from Las Vegas*[2]) and Jencks (*The Language of Postmodern Architecture*[3]) have been far more influential than literary, aesthetic, or philosophical treatments. And certainly we must recognize the pedagogical impact of an expression embodied in buildings and spaces. But all that is not enough: we must also note the architectural turn in aesthetic theory and the extent to which the most important books on postmodernity have made architecture their object of study, seeing it as a matrix for reading the signs of the times. This was the case with a watershed study by Fredric Jameson, *Postmodernism, or The Cultural Logic of Late Capitalism,*[4] which not only dedicated one of its chapters to architecture ("Spatial Equivalents in the World System") but also produced a memorable analysis of the Westin Bonaventure Hotel in Los Angeles.

So we could expect yet another new achievement from architectural theory. After conceptualizing the passage from modernism to postmodernism, would architecture also theorize the passage (although I want to refrain from considering history through a linear, sequential model) from the postmodern to the contemporary? Not with this publication that we're currently studying, because it ignores the postmodern almost entirely (which I'm also doing for the moment, though the topic will come up again later on) to put the contemporary in relationship with modernity. We find that neither of the volume's two authors make any mention of postmodernism, except for a reference to the "bracketed 'post-'"[5]—a helpful phrase, as we shall see later. A periodized view of history is deployed here, which would show postmodernism as a transitional space between "modernisms of the preceding century" and the contemporary, which "can no longer believe in a univocal experience of the physical world, the question of media having become dominant."[6] This thought creates an unexpected displacement of architecture and its relation to media, a displacement that I wish to explore to understand the mediatized element of the contemporary. This element seems important to me, being well aware of the "high price of mediatization through computer screens and television" that we must pay for what Pireyre calls "our experience of the real, whether near or distant."[7]

To help with periodization, Arnaud François, one of the publication's authors, suggests what he calls a "technology of the imagination," which he contrasts with a naturalist imaginary, asserting that if we wish to "grasp the hidden structure of our epoch, dominated by techno-scientific realism, we must become aware of the fact that these representations are structured within latent collective images."[8] From this perspective, it's not relevant to make a distinction between the modern and the contemporary epochs, for they arise from the same ensemble and are characterized by traits of immediacy, synchronization, and simultaneity. These latent collective images are produced by technological images (photography, cinema, television, video, and all computer-aided imagery), and paradoxically, these technology-derived images make us believe in "the possibility of immediate contact with physical reality."

The paradox resides in our imagining that we have the capacity for an *un*-mediated power of perception through mediated images: mediated images and media that, from the nineteenth century to our present day, have never ceased evolving, diversifying, and growing, so much so that one can say that "the imagery of the modern and contemporary eras is technology-derived imagery." This is the volume's most important thesis. The myth rests substantially on a fantasy, always in the process of gaining strength, of a shared temporality, an effective contemporaneity. And now the theoretical importance of these ideas begins to become clearer. The modern and contemporary imaginary is a technological one that can only be understood in terms of contemporaneity. To be in the world assumes a relation, which assumes a sharing in time. To be in the world supposes being-in-time, and to be contemporary supposes a contemporaneity that technological change never stops developing. In this sense, "the contemporary ethos" would very much depend on the very meaning of contemporaneity, because it's based on the capacity to share in time without physical presence. It dissociates (physical) presence and (temporal) simultaneity. This goes some way toward explaining how contemporaneity has slowly become the obsession of an era that strives continually to define it. Arnaud François seems to think this way in the sequential history that he proposes, organized according to the dominant technologies (television, video, computer, and Internet):

> Television, invented in the thirties, began to create a perceptible world in the course of the fifties. . . . For the first time, a technology was able to immediately reproduce an image and diffuse it at once across space. This instantaneous transmission over the airwaves would have phenomenal consequences for contemporary realism. The real would henceforth become assimilated to instantaneousness, and the sense of existence would become tied to constant transfer and movement.
>
> Video, invented in the sixties, in its ability to record the immediate and permanent flux of the television image, encouraged the imagination of a new aesthetic of the real. Memorizing, fixing the electronic image permitted the subjective perception of reaching the interior of the instant, of the flow. The experience of space became that of an accumulation of the flux of the present.
>
> The third stage of the world's recent electronic history arises from the invention of computer images, and almost simultaneously, with that of the Internet.[9]

And yet, according to the author, this third stage is what threatens the very existence of that culmination it was supposed to bring about: the immediacy that was going to give us direct experience of the real via the objective image. With the advent of the computer age, the very meaning of contemporaneity had to be modified: from a sharing of time apart from space, we come to a sharing of temporalities beyond time itself. We move from a contemporaneity of simultaneity to a contemporaneity of synchronization, even of polychronization, insofar as we encounter not substitution but instead addition. This is the trouble with contemporaneity that the contemporary has enabled us to identify. It's no longer a matter of institutions fighting over how to designate the present; instead, it's a matter of inhabiting time and, consequently, space. Again, to be in time, to be in the world, supposes a contemporaneity that these technological mutations have greatly disturbed.

What is the time of the contemporary? What time names or describes the contemporary? These are the questions we must now pose.

SIMULTANEITY AND NATION

If we wish to follow the path taken by our authors, we must first distinguish several of the qualities of contemporaneity brought about by our mediatized relationship to the world. We should speak of qualities rather than phases, for the latter would return us to that sequential vision of history that has become inoperative. These different qualities exist at the same time but, for various reasons, are either dominant or minor. This is the case with the terms *simultaneity* and *synchronization,* which are often used as synonyms for *contemporaneity.* The former returns us to a *euchronic* contemporaneity, to use the term of Georges Didi-Huberman, which I will return to at the end of the present work. The latter takes us to a *synchronic* contemporaneity, which is quite different from Didi-Huberman's vision of contemporaneity as an "extraordinary montage of heterogeneous temporalities that generates anachronisms"[10]—and this latter brings us to the idea of a *polychronic* contemporaneity. All three merit our attention, and all the more so because they do not concern simply our subjective apprehension of the present or, to be more precise, our subjective constitution in the present of relation. Contemporaneity doesn't only constitute the subject; just as profoundly, it constitutes the collective; it establishes the collective through the relation that it institutes. The form of contemporaneity coproduces a type of collective and therefore a political community. This, then, will be our temporary field of investigation. This is where the implicit question resides. What type of political belonging does the contemporary signifier describe?

The historian Benedict Anderson has made some progress toward answering this question. According to him, simultaneity, which is one of the forms of contemporaneity, structures and differentiates the forms of society. To distinguish religious communities, royal dynasties, and nations, he begins by differentiating their apprehension of time and, in particular, their apprehension of simultaneity:

> one could argue that every essential modern conception is based on a conception of "meanwhile."[11]

"Meanwhile" is one of the conceptions of contemporaneity, conceived as simultaneity. This temporal idea of co-presence helps us better understand the larger political modes of structuring and helps us pass more readily from being in time to the forms of society.

The work of Benedict Anderson suggests a theory of the nation from the vantage point of modernity. Now, this organization is one of those that most fully actualizes a certain myth of contemporaneity, one that is no longer ours. A nation (that great accomplishment of modernity) is a massive and anonymous community that fully realizes that its members are not co-present. It ensures a contemporaneity of its members, a sharing in both the present (a simultaneity) and a largely invented history, but its objective is to reinforce contemporaneity. In the 1980s, Benedict Anderson opened up a path for reflection that continues to be explored, and he proposed a kind of anthropology crossed with the imaginary and with technology to distinguish the forms of community as a function of their idea of contemporaneity. In an analysis celebrated for its virtuosity, Anderson focuses on "the elementary structure of two forms of imagining that began to flourish in Europe during the eighteenth century: the novel and the periodical press."[12] Reproducing the plot outline of a Balzacian-style novel, he concludes,

> That all these acts are accomplished at the same calendrical moment, but by actors who are largely unaware of each other shows the novelty of this imagined world that the author has caused to be born in the readers' minds.[13]

The novelty of the world is the (illusory) perception of national simultaneity. The novel enacts and valorizes the simultaneity of society to an extreme, but as a mediatized and technologized object, this simultaneity depends upon the book as a mass-produced artifact of one of the great industrial economies. Let's remember Emmanuelle Pireyre's point about distinguishing the world of the novel and cinema from the world of small screens in our lives: these two worlds not only require different forms of attention but also produce entirely different imagined versions of community.

In its mediatized and technologized form, the great modern press is especially important in concretizing and exemplifying the idea of simultaneity. We only need to pursue Benedict Anderson's ideas and apply them to the topic of artistic representation to see how deeply and how durably the empire of simultaneity and its political figuration—that is, the nation—have taken root, albeit on a short historical scale. We can think, for example, of the novel's narrative techniques that, for a good century, from the mid-nineteenth to the mid-twentieth, sought to create the sense of simultaneity. And we can think of those movements that laid claim to that simultaneity, such as Jules Romains's "unanimism"; and we can think of works by Alfred Döblin or John Dos Passos, and of the pictorial simultaneism of Robert and Sonia Delaunay, and of the poets typically associated with them, like Blaise Cendrars, Guillaume Apollinaire, and Tristan Tzara. Finally, we can think how, since the invention of telephones, radio, and television, the most sought-after programs, no matter the country, were those like the *horloge parlante* (speaking clock) in France—the program or phone number that always offered the exact time.

In short, if Benedict Anderson is correct in thinking that the awareness of a "during this time" marks every form of social organization, the imaginary of the nation (which remains the most important phenomenon of modernity) is constructed with or due to one of its potentialities: simultaneity becomes the primary translation of contemporaneity. We can see a powerful link, almost an essential one, between simultaneity and nation, and we must inquire whether that link remains in place today.

SYNCHRONIZATION, POLYCHRONICITY, ETHNOSCAPE, AND GLOBALIZATION

In part, it was radio and television, the great mass media of the twentieth century, that radicalized or pushed to the extreme and even transformed that simultaneism so important to modernism. For, if the modern novel could only represent simultaneity and insist on an awareness of it, and if the modern press could produce a daily simultaneity within the space of reception, the newer media insist on a co-occurrence between broadcast and reception—regardless of the kind of program being broadcast. Whether live or prerecorded, both radio and television employ this concordance between emission and reception. Obviously, from the point of view of temporality, the other forms of simultaneity that we've encountered cannot effect this synchronization between emission and reception of message. But this form of contemporaneity as simultaneity is disrupted with the invention of new technologies that put into play a new possibility: the synchronization/desynchronization of the present. First we have the advent of the recording technologies, notably video, which allows for a desynchronization of emission and reception and an upheaval in the flow of time controlled by radio and television. We can replay the present when it is past.

A large part of video art is based on this principle. Added to the simultaneous contemporary (that which produces the idea of the nation) and to the synchronic contemporary (that which produces supranational communities founded on the principle of homogeneity—if indeed this effect is ever attained) is a polychronic contemporary (that which produces the idea of globalization—though this, too, needs further verification). This should be considered an addition because, first, it's not a matter of substituting one medium for another but rather of their coexistence and, second, because each of the media is altered by the unique quality of contemporaneity of the others. This addition is reinforced by the development of information and communication technologies, especially the Internet, which possess all the qualities of contemporaneity—not only simultaneity and synchronization/desynchronization but above all polychronization. If we posit that simultaneity is the contemporaneity of nations, and synchronicity that of large assemblages, and polychronicity that of globalization, then we are living in a time of superimposed contemporaneities. This hypermediatized contemporaneity thus falls under the heading of more than one concordance of temporalities—a concordance more subjective than collective. Or to put it another way, it's less *a* present—a single, unique, and unified present—that we share as members of a community and more a subjectivized polychronicity. Furthermore, a very large part of contemporary literary and artistic production has inscribed its place of imagination within this polychronicity. Just as fascination with simultaneity marked the early twentieth century (and with it a manifest fascination with the idea of the nation), a fascination with communitarian synchronicity and subjective, performative polychronicity marks the turning of the twenty-first century. This has had profound political consequences.

The Indian anthropologist Arjun Appadurai has thoroughly discussed this point.[14] Those who have read him will no doubt recall the example he gives in his conclusion (and this links him to the Balzacian simultaneism studied by Anderson): the Pakistani taxi drivers in Chicago who "listen to cassettes of sermons recorded in mosques in Pakistan or Iran."[15] Among Appadurai's most striking ideas is his insistence on recordings over different times and their impact on synchronization/desynchronization considered as a process of detachment from the model of the Nation-State, to the benefit of transnational communities, and notably the *ethnoscapes* that are his chief interest. After Appadurai's book, words formed with the suffix -*scape* are used to designate the transnational distribution of correlated elements that form environments. The *ethnoscapes* refer less to ethnic origin than to human communities, and they must be distinguished from *mediascapes, technoscapes,* and *financescapes.* The idea helps Appadurai think about all the forms of community for which national attachment is an insufficient descriptor—such as migrants, tourists, diasporas; the growth of such forms is one characteristic of the contemporary. Appadurai adapts Benedict Anderson's idea that the various forms of community are largely imaginary, produced within a particular media-driven environment, a *mediascape,* which itself implies a form of contemporaneity. But he doesn't explicitly pursue Anderson's reflections on the relationship that supports the forms of community and the nature of the contemporaneity that links them together. Yet implicitly, Appadurai evokes the three forms of contemporaneity we have been exploring: simultaneism, synchronization, polychronism. It is the nature of the contemporaneity that distinguishes the three modes of collective identity: simultaneity and the nation; the synchronization of supranational forms of community founded on a homogeneity (imaginary, of course), and notably the *ethnoscapes* that become visible through recording and diffusion; and the polychronicity of globalization in a hypermediatized world that creates the co-existence of all forms of temporality. The notion of the neighbor or the neighborhood so important for Appadurai should also be understood in its temporal dimension of co-temporality, which, of course, constitutes the primary meaning of *contemporary,* from the temporal point of view. The key word for our first series was *indistinction,* and the key word for our second is *co-temporality.* The contemporary emerges as a historical category in taking on these two ideas.

One more point about the political consequences of this temporal concept. Subjective polychronism differentiates itself from national simultaneism and supranational synchronization in that it produces, not communities, but rather performative and temporary subjects. In the same way, publics are differentiated from communities precisely because the former are performative, temporary, and nonexclusive, whereas the latter are considered permanent, exclusive, and essential. The era of hypermedia did not invent this kind of political stratification: in the seventeenth century, to be Bourguignon, a merchant, French, and Catholic likewise, implied a similar stratification. But the mediatized imaginary of the contemporary reveals the fictional quality of the idea of a unitary community (whether national, transnational, or supranational), one incarnated in a single media-driven environment producing its own contemporaneity and its political community. This new imaginary transforms the form *community* into the form *public.* As a result, belonging to a nation is likewise seen as performative and temporary. This is why the field of political research today has turned (not exclusively, of course, but very largely) toward subjective constructions, not as a retreat to singularity but as a performative archive that brings with it conflicts of definition. Contemporary contemporaneity is what allows us to dissolve the unitary fiction conveyed by a dominant *mediascape*. It's what brings many mediatized contemporaneities into being.

ATTENTION AND THE "LITERARY BRAIN"

It also makes us exist within those numerous mediatized contemporaneities. What time are we living in? The answer is difficult when the question is posed in the singular. We are living in many times simultaneously. And this profusion is going to grow in the hypermediatized environments that form what we will call the "attention economy." The contemporaneity of mediatized times demands more and more precious capital—our attention—which can be invested simultaneously in several temporal realms, each of which, as we have seen, carries with it its own ideology. The company of screens, as Emmanuelle Pireyre says, is often difficult, because it's a company that prefers distraction to attention and immersion. One of the most discussed texts of the last decade concerned exactly this subject: "Is Google Making Us Stupid?"[16] by Nicholas Carr, which centers on the author's anxiety over his inability to devote prolonged attention to things that demand it, in this case, books. This inability comes from his exposure to the Internet. Less peremptory than it might seem, the text envisages the end of an era marked by the preeminence of the literary brain, of which one of the chief attributes was hyperattentiveness, the capacity for profound attention. New media and technologies are not seen simply as tools but as reconfigurations of our relationship to the world that can, according to Nicholas Carr, lead to neuronal reconfigurations. It goes without saying, and this has been proven by all media theory, that every new medium has the ability to reorient the ensemble of media within its own configuration. Carr develops the double image of the scuba diver and the driver of a Jet Ski. The era he calls "literary" was a time of the deep scuba dive, with a dominant temporal modality; the time of the Internet is the Jet Ski era, skipping from wave to wave, from temporality to temporality. However, the metaphor needs to be a bit more nuanced. The Jet Ski does not substitute for the deep dive; rather, it's an addition. This is what *contemporary* means: no substitutions, only additions. Of course, our hypermediatized contemporaneity is indeed marked by a crisis of attention, one that has only worsened. But we are not hopelessly condemned to a crisis of attention.

Yves Citton has explained how one can move from an economy of attention to an ecology of attention.[17] The ecology of attention is an ecology of temporalities, an awareness of their resources. The contemporary is at the heart of this dynamic: to be contemporary is, above all, to experience the contemporaneity of solicitations on our attention. The performative element is important here: the multiplicity of media is such that it's possible for us, much more than it was in the era of the great dominant forms of media, to shift or vary our attention, pluralize it, inhabit it, individualize it, with a complete awareness that the flow it processes is collective—"none of which prevents us from living in it," Pireyre adds. There are many modes of being mediatized. Becoming spellbound is one, of course. But awakening from the spell is also one of the modes. And this awakening arises in large part from an awareness of the multiplicity of temporalities that we inhabit. Certain attentional experiences form a kind of laboratory for ways of being in time. An exemplary case is that of aesthetic experiences. Yves Citton writes,

> Knowing how to choose our alienations and our enthrallments, knowing how to establish vacuoles of silence capable of protecting us from the incessant communication that overloads us with crushing information, knowing how to inhabit switches between

> hyper-focusing and hypo-focusing—this is what aesthetic expe-
> riences (experiences with music, cinema, theater, literature, or
> videogames) can help to do with our attention, since attention
> is always just as much something that we *do* (by ourselves) as it
> is something that we *pay* (to another).[18]

This is not a matter of resacralizing aesthetic experiences, and in any case, in Citton's view, the aesthetic experiences produced by cultural industries (television series or video games, for example) have the same value as those produced by the venerable literary experience, but they allow one to create those "vacuoles" as protection against the assaults of communication while being fully familiar with them. In addition, they permit one to manage the three principal modes in which one can be of our time, be contemporary: hyperattention, floating attention, and standby. This was the problem Emmanuelle Pireyre discussed in her "Fictions documentaires." From a literary point of view, she drew a distinction between the kinds of attention demanded by "vacuole" experiences (novel, cinema, theater) and "compositionist" experiences (documentary fictions). Many other experiences are possible, and we need not reestablish some aesthetic hierarchy—far from it. Rather, we need to enlarge our idea of the aesthetic experience, to find it within microcommunities, within small groups (Roland Barthes), in attention to the other (i.e., care); all of these can help us when our attention is threatened. Contrary to what those who believe there has been a decline in attention think, these performative laboratories of attention have never been as numerous as they are today, nor have they been as widely shared.

AN ARCHAEOLOGY OF MEDIA

This multiplication brings with it a change in the hermeneutic paradigm of our idea of time and thus in the history of forms. Curiously, with the entry into a hypermediatized time, cultural critique, faced with such simultaneity, such co-presence, but also with such constant obsolescence, needs to examine inverse topics: residualities, spectralities, archaeology, polychronicity. Studies devoted to the most recent and sometimes the most ephemeral mutations become fertile fields for the most intense archaeological analyses. Thus the modern sense of the history of forms conceived as a permanent substitution for obsolescences is entirely inverted.

There are two main reasons for this. Observing the media is the best way to see the cumulative (not substitutive) nature of temporality. The computer did not replace the telephone, and electronic messaging did not replace either of them. Each works with a temporality proper to its own co-presence, and these temporalities are superimposed upon each other. Because they suggest a permanent obsolescence, there is a felt need to document them in quasi-real time. The entire history of forms—inherited, successive, substitutive—all of them are overthrown.

But at the same time, our cultural theory inherits the pioneering work carried out by Walter Benjamin, who opened up a hitherto unknown field of inquiry, the cultural archaeology of the contemporary; Benjamin established the rules of the game and furnished the mode of historical interpretation that is best suited for our epoch (a mode to which the present study is much indebted). The closer one comes to the present of cultural representations, the more one becomes charged with multiple, sedimented values, and the more one's approach becomes an archaeological one. It is always the same image, used even in antiquity: is our present the oldest or the newest of times? The archaeological image opts for the former, because our present is thick with all those pasts.

Benjamin's intellectual gesture is fundamental for the study of the contemporary. Not that others before him had not been interested in contemporary cultural productions, but the earlier thinkers worked within a traditional cultural framework, reducing their field of inquiry to artistic practices. Benjamin is the first to have taken a materialist approach to cultural and artistic productions, taking their mediatized nature into account, that is to say, their capacity for establishing a contact, for opening up a synchronization. Everyone knows Benjamin's "The Work of Art in the Age of Technological Reproducibility," but we must remember that this was preceded by his "Little History of Photography" as well as numerous texts on the cinema, radio[19] (a medium with which he also engaged intensely), and the telephone. The title of his (all too brief) magnum opus on the question indicates his historical orientation very clearly: how does the present of "technologies of reproducibility" transform the "work of art," which was supposed to exist outside of time? The revolutionary moments in Benjamin's work are legion: first, stressing the materiality of artifacts; next, seeing objects linked to mass consumption; but above all, for our purposes, making the present the only observation post possible. That is, Benjamin's essay rejects the historical perspectives of sequential succession in favor of an archaeological approach, in which we can read the traces of the past in the forms of the present. This is a double revolution (not axiological but methodological): in favor of the contemporary, and in favor of the archaeological perspective. But this double upheaval is effected in a single movement. This is because our only observation post is the present, and as a result of that, historical inquiry is archaeological; that is, it takes into account the polychronicity of each present.

This nonstandard vision of history was left unexplored for several decades before cultural critique began to make use of it. But with our entry into a hypermediatized era over these last thirty or forty years, it has come to inform almost the entirety of the field. As evidence of this, the body of "media studies" has increasingly become a body of "media archaeology." Recently, one of these new archaeologists has offered a book of synthesis[20] that recalls the idea, so important in the present study, that "archaeology is always, implicitly or explicitly, an archaeology of the present"; the analysis of media, considered as a theory of the present, fits within the group of alternative and nonlinear histories, the harbingers of which were probably Walter Benjamin and Aby Warburg.

There is another lesson that cultural critique can draw from a mediatized approach to contemporaneity. Formerly (and of course using that word "formerly" does not imply a homogeneity), the critique of works, especially works about then contemporary artworks like those of Giorgio Vasari or Denis Diderot, like those of Pliny the Elder, even if, strictly speaking, there was no continuity between them, were integrated into a system of perpetuation. The various artistic practices seemed to form a system that existed "since time immemorial," in which its metamorphoses were less spectacular than its permanences.

With the entry of the mediatized age (the nineteenth century) and then the hypermediatized age (the second half of the twentieth century) came an unheard-of connection between forms and experiences: the documentation not of a perpetuation but of numerous births—of photography, the phonograph, the cinema, television, the Internet, and all the forms of life that they brought with them. One can point to a date, at least a symbolic one, for the birth of the cinematograph: December 28, 1895, at the Salon Indien in Paris.[21] That day, a number of reporters and journalists witnessed and documented the event.[22] Many elements must be taken into account here. With the appearance of new ways of seeing and hearing using new technical processes,[23] the meaning of contemporaneity changed. Even though new modes of literary and art criticism were applied to contemporary works, it was the works of art and the criticism concerning them that were inevitably seen as being in tune with "new media." Whether in a positive or negative manner, literary works and criticism remained within a system of perpetuation, one they could not really change; but the latter, works of art and art criticism, helped in the process of altering the history of forms. They became the emblematic phenomena of their era. And as emblems, they represented their contemporaneity.

The media archaeology of our own era, and at the basis of the ensemble of theoretical perspectives, tends to include artistic and cultural practices within the media system. This displacement insists on their nature as methods of communication (and thus of synchronization, sometimes even of simultaneity).

In this way, we can see how the contemporary appearance of new ways of seeing and hearing profoundly modifies and reframes (i.e., deterritorializes or reterritorializes) the ensemble of artistic and cultural productions. This is the point Walter Benjamin also made with the idea of technological reproducibility, which allowed him to turn to the history of cultural forms. For example, we can recall these statements from the first pages of "The Work of Art in the Age of Its Technological Reproducibility":

> In principle, the work of art has always been reproducible.... The enormous changes brought about in literature by movable type, the technological reproduction of writing, are well known. But they are only a special case, though an important one, of the phenomenon considered here from the perspective of world history....
>
> Around 1900, technological reproduction not only had reached a standard that permitted it to reproduce all known works of art, profoundly modifying their effect, but it also had captured a place of its own among the artistic processes. In gauging this standard, we would do well to study the impact which its two different manifestations—the reproduction of artworks and the art of film—are having on art in its traditional form.[24]

The present acts like a key to the past, to multiple pasts, to temporalities. This is the Benjaminian "lesson" drawn by media theory; it profoundly informs both the contemporary approach to time and the approach to time as essentially contemporary—that is, time that can only live since the advent of the contemporary.

DISJUNCTION OF TEMPORALITIES

The first series concluded on the importance of space, especially public space. And it involved institutional history. But the contemporary is also a temporal issue. To invert the earlier proposition, we could easily say that to inhabit the same space is also to share a time, a contemporaneity. Contemporaneity is immediately a political issue because it constitutes communities, or at least relations. Now, contemporaneity is not homogeneous, nor is it unique; many types of contemporaneity exist, forming many types of communities— many types of communities which, moreover, have been steeped in political discourse. The proximity of individual subjects is not in itself sufficient to produce a sense of community once we, as individuals, begin to experience a sense of belonging to much larger conceptions of communities beyond the neighborhood, thanks to a contemporaneity produced simultaneously by processes and a mediatized imaginary. We can therefore establish a link between the technological imaginary, forms of political subjectivity, and a relation to contemporaneity. Benedict Anderson has clearly shown how the national imaginary was tied to the spread of the novel and the larger world of publishing, both the one and the other creating the illusion of a simultaneity within a tightly linked community. The anthropologist Arjun Appadurai has pursued the topic for supranational communities by insisting not on simultaneity but on the possibility of controlling the flow of time while replaying it, thanks to recording (audio or video cassettes), which synchronizes those whom simultaneity can no longer unite, notably diasporic communities. There is a fundamental link between what he calls *ethnoscape* and *mediascape*. In that case, two contemporaneities can enter into conflict. But a third form of contemporaneity must be envisioned, linked to the hypermediatized world: that of the polychronicity of temporalities themselves, which articulate diverse forms of simultaneity and which produce and participate in a globalized imaginary. For the appearance of new media (and with them new political imaginaries of shared time) does not lead to the disappearance of the old. The contemporaneity of the hyper-mediatized era is the articulation, the negotiation, often agonistic, of numerous mediatized imaginaries that correspond to forms of political communities: national, supranational, global. An agonistic negotiation is in itself a political one, if one agrees with the ideas of Chantal Mouffe, who connects the analysis of public spaces with politics and conflict, notably through her idea of agonistic pluralism.[25]

All the popular uprisings, all the revolts and revolutions of these recent years, arise from a disjunction of temporalities. Derrida quoted Shakespeare: "The time is out of joint."[26] Much has been said about the revolutions produced by social media. Those who have lived through them have felt, dramatically, the confrontation between the forms of temporal communities produced by state media, support from supranational recordings, and the superimposition of the temporalities of social media. The contemporary, the world we call "contemporary"—and perhaps this is the reason we call it that—is characterized by a proliferation of unexpected forms of contemporaneity. This is why political questions get transferred to the level of subjectivities. The contemporary *mediascape* produces not communities but rather publics that are performative, temporary, nonexclusive, while modern *mediascapes* engendered an imaginary of permanent communities, exclusive and essentialized. Or, to put it another way, these communities, within the mediatized contemporary and its forms of contemporaneity, are not nullified but rather in competition with those performative and temporary publics. The hypermediatized moment makes numerous contemporaneities coexist, and they can be in conflict with each other. These conflicts play out in contemporary subjectivity. Let's conclude with these words by Emmanuelle Pireyre:

If the relationship with the world is not an open antagonism between the I and exterior reality, but rather a slippage, a movement from the I into the phenomena of social discourse, with the desire to borrow from them, to reconfigure them, to make them intersect with the interior world, to make them habitable— then, the attention is displaced toward the plural, toward social constructions, toward extensions of Ourselves in variable dimensions.[27]

Publication

THE UNTIMELY AND CONTEMPORANEITY: VENICE, 2005

With the third occurrence of our question—what is the contemporary?—we're changing both the nature of the question and our altitude. We began with fanzines, manifestos, more or less limited publications, but now we find ourselves in the world of one the great "stars" of critical theory.

Giorgio Agamben, now entering our arena, is a thinker of worldwide reputation, a reputation earned through the originality of his approaches and the topics he chooses to address. In describing his work, one could say he isn't a modern philosopher in the conventional sense of the term but in the sense that he restores philological, religious, and juridical commentary and exegesis to its heuristic mode, and does so with the topics most salient to our contemporaneity. In 2008, when *Che cos'è il contemporaneo?* was published, his books from *Homo Sacer* onward had already installed Agamben in that rarified intellectual class created by the international university system, under the hegemony of the United States. But unlike the majority of such stars, perhaps unlike any of his peers, Agamben has remained somewhat on the margins of the movement by refusing to come to the United States following the country's adoption of biometric passports, an example of the political situation of the "state of exception" that his books discuss.

To my knowledge, his book on the concept of the contemporary is the first time a philosopher of such renown posed an ontological question since Deleuze and Guattari's book *What Is Philosophy?*[1] And it's the first time that the contemporary found itself the subject of international intellectual discussion, after discussions that took place at local levels in Rosario and Rouen. With the release of Agamben's book, nothing would be the same again. We are thus indebted to Agamben for making the word's substantive form into a historical identifier.

The publication took two forms, one dramatic and the other more understated. First was the simultaneous publication in Italy and France of a tiny book. The simultaneity signals that this was an event. We are well aware of the reception that these sorts of books are accorded. If a publisher is willing to cover the costs of editing, printing, distribution, and publicity, it must be because he or she has decided it's worth the trouble—and worth it to the extent that another publisher in a different language, bearing the translation costs, is willing to participate in the event.[2]

What do we learn from this short text, almost as poetic as it is philosophical? Or rather, since the book is cited more often than it is read, what has been taken from it by those who have declared it an essential text on theories of the contemporary? It falls firmly in the Nietzschean tradition of a paradoxical passion for the present—the tradition that begins with Nietzsche's *Unzeitgemässe Betrachtungen,* a title difficult to translate: *Untimely Meditations*; *Considérations inactuelles*; *Considerazioni inattuali* . . . (Only the Italian and French stress *inactualité,* the untimely, the state of not being of the present moment.) The tradition shows a passion for the present on the condition that the present is not identified with the current, not with the time that is passing now. The two theses from the text most often repeated are these: there is a *true* contemporary, and it is untimely. This is what distinguishes the "true" contemporary from being simply the time that is passing now, from currentness.

Because we're dealing with a somewhat prophetic text, it rejects all logical development and any kind of argument, remaining instead—as fascinating as they are irritating—a series of startling assertions. Sentences can be quoted from it to demonstrate the prose of the epoch, like the following:

> Those who are truly contemporary, who truly belong to their time, are those who neither perfectly coincide with it nor adjust themselves to its demands. They are thus in this sense irrelevant [*inattuale*]. But precisely because of this condition, precisely through this disconnection and this anachronism, they are more capable than others of perceiving and grasping their own time.[3]

Or the following, which is repeated insistently in practically every discussion of the contemporary:

> The contemporary is one who is struck and startled by the beam of darkness that comes from his own time.[4]

But have we really understood this text—and the connection between these two quoted sentences? The book is Agamben's lecture given at the opening of his seminar, and that lecture was important in that it disengaged the contemporary from being seen as epochal, choosing instead to see it as a theory of the event. "The 'time' of our seminar is contemporariness," he wrote.[5] Contemporaneity is inscribed in the exigencies of act and of relation, not in the description of objects. The emblematic act, according to him, is that of reading, which allows us to coinhabit disjointed worlds and temporalities.

But most importantly, at the very beginning of his seminar, Agamben responds to a supposed objection from his public (who later became his readership), not hesitating at all to use the direct copulative verb for his simple definition of the contemporary: "the contemporary is the untimely."[6] To prevent this formula from appearing to be a slogan, we must embed it within its context:

> An initial, provisional indication that may orient our search for an answer to the above questions comes from Nietzsche. Roland Barthes summarizes this answer in a note from his lectures at the Collège de France: "The contemporary is the untimely."[7]

The triple authority—Nietzsche/Barthes/Agamben—is important, and so is the slogan, but we must also attend to some other key terms: *indication, provisional, orient, inquiry.* Discussing Nietzsche but without making use of Nietzsche's German text, Agamben—who is perfectly at ease with German—returns to the untimely nature of the contemporary condition, presenting it not as a distancing or a flight from the present but as a noncoinciding, an unsynching, a nonagreement:

> Contemporariness is, then, a singular relationship with one's own time, which adheres to it and, at the same time, keeps a distance from it. More precisely, it is *that relationship with time that adheres to it through a disjunction and an anachronism.* Those who coincide too well with the epoch, those who are perfectly tied to it in every respect, are not contemporaries, precisely because they do not manage to see it; they are not able to firmly hold their gaze on it.[8]

The question seems to have evolved. It is no longer "what is the contemporary?" nor "in what time are we living?" as before; instead, it has now become "who are contemporaries?" The conceptual horizon of this question arises from the literature of the nineteenth century, and especially from French literature from Chateaubriand to Stendhal, by way of Baudelaire. A double question is posed, political and literary, one we have not seen much of since the Rosario brouhaha, but one of those that determines the contemporary. To the extent that dynamic democracy puts more and more persons into the political scene, can one consider all these people as true actors or agents? To the extent that historical temporality now centers on the present and no longer on the past, what can the writers or historians do, now that they're engaged in the events they used to stand apart from and document? Can one be fully engaged and also fully understand? Aren't there two kinds of agents: the first kind, who understand, and the second, who simply act? These are questions that allow us to distinguish contemporaneity from currentness. According to the study by Vincent Descombes (another philosopher who has grappled with the question of the contemporary), these are the questions that motivated Chateaubriand, author of *Memoirs from beyond the Tomb*, when he attempted to describe the revolutionary events of July 1830. The following is the passage Descombes cites in his article,[9] which constitutes a foundational text for the theory of the untimely:

> I have described the three days as they unfolded before me; there is a certain contemporary coloring, which seems true at the moment it occurs but false once the moment has passed, and this affects my description. There is no revolution so prodigious that, if it were described from one minute to the next, would not become reduced to the smallest proportions. Events are born from the womb of things, like men from the wombs of their mothers, accompanied by all the weaknesses of nature. Miseries and grandeurs are twins, born together; but though the labor pains are harsh, the miseries die away after a while, and only the grandeurs live on. To judge impartially the facts that remain, one must adopt the point of view from which posterity will judge the complete event.[10]

This passage from Chateaubriand constitutes the intellectual matrix in which Agamben's text is inscribed. Asynchronicity and anachronism can be understood as the point of view of that posterity, the only one among the actors—but the real problem is, which posterity will it be?—capable of seeing (and this seeing is not so much a matter of vision as one of clairvoyance, it would seem). Chateaubriand's text is more explicit than Agamben's, disqualifying the "simple" present from the present that has become past and thus has become posterity, which is the ensemble of imperfections, of fine grain, of those "smallest proportions," those "miseries." What the actors themselves live is an unfiltered whole, unpurified, unselected, and those who write the chronicle cannot know that whole. For there are two, apparently contradictory propositions: the present is the fully mature historical temporality; it is impossible to make literature or legend out of it. Much of the literature of the nineteenth century is devoted to this apparent contradiction. Stendhal's scene of Fabrizio at Waterloo can stand as its emblem.

But why is it that when we are in the present, we cannot see it properly? There are two reasons, at least according to Descombes's reading of Chateaubriand. First, as we have seen, because the miseries (which memory must eliminate) and the grandeurs (which must be conserved for posterity) are mixed together. The epoch must contain both some things that are meaningful and some that are insignificant ("the miseries die away after a while, and only the grandeurs live on"). But meaningful for whom? We now come to the second proposition. The "historians of the present" (the phrase is from Descombes) see nothing because they share in the same passions as the actors. They are in an affective relation to the present, therefore, and this is what blinds them. "All eras, for those who experience contemporariness, are obscure," says Agamben.[11]

Thus the only ones who can find the meaning of the epoch are those who abstract themselves from those passions. As Descombes puts it,

> thus the "color of contemporaneity" arises from the passions of the historians of the present, passions they share with the actors. This means that there is an affective modality proper to

the contemporary. The passions felt by the actors are the passions of the contemporaries, for these passions are born from
the affairs that are not yet resolved, events which are in process
but not yet concluded.[12]

This approach is precisely my antimodel. I think it may even allow
us to distinguish between a modern way and a contemporary way
of comprehending the present. For the latter, this comprehension is
born out of an engagement with the triviality of the present. There
are indeed two different paths taken by studies of contemporary
phenomena: the one supposes a certain distance, a kind of view
from above, a detachment, an abstraction, but also a distinction;
the other is embedded, contemporary in the third sense of the term
(a comrade of the time), compositionist, materialist, egalitarian,
and it accepts the risk of "blindness."

Agamben's text is thus based on this double distinction, between
actors and capacities, quite the contrary to what we saw in the cases
of Rosario and Rouen. This basis is reinforced by two fragments
that follow. As Alain Badiou did in order to read the "century,"[13]
Agamben turns to a poem by Osip Mandelstam on the assump-
tion both theorists make, that poetry is a discourse of truth, not
to say *the* discourse of truth. One notes the slippage that occurs
from one of Agamben's phrasings to the other: "the poet, insofar
as he is contemporary,"[14] becomes "the poet—the contemporary,"[15]
the em dash signaling an equivalence. Thus we must now turn
to Baudelaire, for whom the figure of the poet exists in a state of
exceptionality, enjoying incomparable privileges, to paraphrase his
prose poem "The Crowds" ("Les foules"). And those privileges are
equally sacrifices, to paraphrase Mandelstam. The centrality of the
literary in Agamben is surprising, considering how the centrality of
literature is constantly lessening in our world. It rests on a distinctive
imaginary of literature—or rather, of Literature with a capital *L*—
and upon the knowledge structurations and social structurations

that this imaginary assumes. Jean-Marie Schaeffer's analysis can help, as he explores the so-called crisis in literature and attempts to uncover its origins:

> People tend . . . to reduce "literary culture" to one of its institutional representations, according to which Literature appears as an autonomous reality, a closed system of its own. This canonical vision was established by the *separationist* model of the nineteenth century, and it continues largely to shape our current representations of literature.[16]

There would seem to be, therefore, an untimely quality to Literature, one founded on a "literary absolute" with regard to the culture which provides its most intimate context. The "separationist" model described by Jean-Marie Schaeffer is precisely the distinctive model I evoked earlier and called "modern." It explains that startling return to distinction and verticality, as opposed to horizontality and the affirmation of equality to which our first investigation of contemporaneity led us.

At least this is true at the beginning of Agamben's text. What follows seems like a course reversal. We might get the impression that among that play of light and shadow that characterizes the present in Agamben's view, our attention should have been directed toward the lights and the stars. This is the distinctive hypothesis on which we have been working. But as the text proceeds, being contemporary consists of "a neutralization of the lights that come from the epoch in order to discover its obscurity, its special darkness, which is not, however, separable from those lights."[17] On the contrary, this approach is archaeological. The visible arises from the depths of obscurity, which is all that matters. At best, the illuminations can only provide a point of access for the depths that they witness. We can see how this approach disturbs that modernist, literature-centered reading and how it resonates with the theoretical position underlying the ensemble of propositions we have encountered in our inquiry. Not only is the present now visible but visibility and invisibility are no longer in opposition, for they are of the same nature. Thanks to his turn to "contemporary astrophysics,"[18] Agamben manages to describe both the emergent and the submerged, the apparent and the hidden, as the same phenomenon in different states—temporary, reversible states. This approach unites two perspectives of cultural theory. It's no longer a matter of canonizing or classicizing contemporary phenomena, as in some literary studies, nor is it a matter of picking out the stars—the "great author" or the "great artist"—but neither is it a matter of using a sociological or quantitative approach; rather, it's a matter of establishing a state of the visible together with the invisible. Most commentators skip over this part of Agamben's text to maintain only the distinctive thesis concerning the imaginary of Literature, which is not merely the modern imaginary but much more, the very emblem of modernity.

EXHIBITING LITERATURE: PANTIN, 2007

In parallel to this, a different imaginary evolved out of literature itself, one more in phase with the characteristics of the contemporary. This imaginary is that of publication, which forms a veritable dialectic with Literature, a dialectic that interests me not only because I am a literary theorist but also because it reveals the differences between the modern and the contemporary. The idea emerged from a project I had initiated, titled "What Is the Contemporary?" (the fourth occurrence of the question), in 2007 in Paris and Seine-Saint-Denis. I bring up this project because it had three distinct layers: a literary program within a departmental network of municipal libraries; a first publication of a periodical of independent creative and critical work, whose authors responded to the work by two sound artists, resulting in a multimedia work; and a university colloquium followed by publication in book form.

Literature in the public space, in digital space, and in a volume: the three iterations of the one project.

The network of municipal libraries is to the great research libraries what art centers are to museums: new public spaces that have become essential to literature. Such a network is essential for writers, for it allows them to earn income based on authors' rights. It's essential for political institutions, because it justifies the idea of cultural practices as social vector, as socially important. It's essential for the whole literary world, which is excessively stratified, to welcome a new wave of writers and other actors (literary advisors and intermediaries) who have had to invent new materialities for literature apart from the book. "Encountering literature in books has become almost a rarity," I wrote with Olivia Rosenthal in 2010, in an attempt to describe what we began calling "exhibited literature."[19] Writers who want to be visible *as* writers must find ways to make themselves visible. Their interventions in social media work together with a literary cultural industry in which the physical presence of the author is increasingly required: from public lectures and signings in bookstores to helping plan and hold large literary festivals, we are witnessing a transformation in the social presence of the author. The writer's visibility has become both an aesthetic principle and a social condition.

This cultural swing takes us far from the imaginary of Literature, which becomes even more evident in the second part of the project: the audio issue of the magazine *Chaoïd,* by Jean-Jacques Palix and Ève Couturier. The magazine is a witness to encounters within the library, because it made recordings of them there.[20] But it placed them within an audio creation that employs all the effects we associate with artistic intention: cutting, suspension, doubling, assembling, recomposing, playing with sound and words, and so on. And it did all this within the framework of a literary magazine on the Internet, which in itself has overdetermined its aesthetic intention. It is notable too that the issue was presented at a public soirée—in contrast to a simple book launch at a bookstore.

This cultural swing is quite typical of the contemporary conditions of literature, which call into question "the condition of the writer we have seen described over the last two centuries: we have been given the image of the author, a recluse in his office or studio, working in direct relation with his publisher and the actors who populate the field (critics, literary juries, etc.), speaking *in absentia* to a mass, anonymous audience."[21] From meetings in libraries to literature on the Internet, the project "What Is the Contemporary?" revealed this new exhibition aspect of literature. The third leg of the project is more traditional, because it involves a university colloquium, bringing together authors and researchers primarily from the literary field. But classic as it was, the colloquium (which I codirected with Zahia Rahmani and Tiphaine Samoyault) nevertheless situated itself outside the closed world of the university, at the National Center for Dance, in Pantin, a location emblematic of the politics of decentralizing culture into the Parisian *banlieues*, and thus also emblematic of the transformation of public spaces that we have already encountered. The different sections of the colloquium reveal the orientation clearly: a terminological approach and a geopolitical approach. While discussion was very much in the form of dialogue, there was still a detectable guiding thread: the need to historicize an idea, contemporaneity, that was presented as "weak, but yet with a weak intensity," to territorialize it through cultural geopolitics, the objective being to remove the "Western" centrality of the concept and to maintain and reclaim a currentness as opposed to a classicization of the contemporary. Most of the key theoretical issues were aired during the meetings. But what most interests me here is the scheme itself: most of the participants were writers and literary theorists, but they were not in the location one would expect—theorists were speaking in a choreographic and media center, and writers had emerged from their offices and studios, departing from the model of Literature *in absentia* to show themselves in public spaces, *in praesentia*.

LITERATURE-SILENCE VERSUS LITERATURE-BROUHAHA

Agamben's text and the Pantin project suggest two literary imaginaries and, along with them, two imaginaries of being in a developing historical time. The two imaginaries largely align with the
recurrent distinction between the public sphere and public space.
The Literature imaginary deploys an immaterial, abstract sphere,
whereas exhibited literature inhabits public spaces. Some readers will recognize that I'm borrowing a distinction from Jürgen
Habermas, who, not content with having produced an archaeology
of the emergence of bourgeois society, has contributed more than
anyone else to the analysis of the literary imaginary as constitutive
of modern societies. Since his book in 1962,[22] he places contemporary literature, and contemporaneity, at the heart of his system.

The objective of Habermas's book is to analyze the establishment of a new political conception concerning the foundation of
modern European societies. To do this, he lays out a distinction
between the public domain (the domain of the State, of power) and
the private domain (that of individuals). In premodern absolutist
regimes, the public domain is entirely privatized by a caste whose
private domain is itself public. This is the famous formula of Louis
XIV: "L'état, c'est moi." But what remains for the rest of the population is an entirely private existence. According to Habermas, in
Germany, England, and France, the growth of bourgeois society
was accompanied by a split in the private domain, between a private
sphere and a "political public" sphere, in which private persons
assemble to discuss issues of public or common interest.

According to Habermas, literature plays a determinative role
in the constitution of this public sphere. It's because of this space
opening for debate about contemporary art and especially literature in the eighteenth century that the foundations of a political
public sphere came to be sketched out. An urban public followed
the courtly public, especially with the growth of salons and their

offspring, the cafés, "in which began to emerge, between aristocratic society and bourgeois intellectuals, a certain parity of the educated."[23] Of course, this is an idealized construction in which "people" in the cafés are "bourgeois" men, an equality that operates within a new dominant class. Habermas is not so much tracing a reality as performing the archaeology of an ideology that was imposed upon reality. The imprint was received and passed on as if it were reality.

Nevertheless, this ideology imposed on reality reveals to us that the literary debate existed before the political one and thus before the public sphere. For this forum is only a step in a much larger process, which is the transformation of the agora into society, via the marketplace. For Habermas, this nuclear model cannot close upon itself, art itself having become merchandise. It must expand to constitute a true public sphere no longer possible within public spaces. This is the idea of the "general public," which must not be confused with a country's population or, even less, with the people. The question we have asked before arises again: how are communities that share the same time constituted—that is, how are they imagined? The "general public" is educated by the school system and above all by the critical discourse used in the newspapers and magazines, whose empire dates from this time. Physical gatherings become a thing of the past: "The public that read and debated [the topics in the periodicals] read and debated about itself."[24] There exists, then, a superior encounter or assembly, within the immaterial public sphere.

It was clear from our very first series that the representation of public space and the theory of the contemporary go hand in hand. There is no constitution of communities, groups, publics, masses, or classes, except as a function of a certain conception of sharing in a time. And a very powerful one is to be found informing the theories of modernity, centered on the idealized model of the literary encounter.

This is because the influential model that Habermas analyzes, the one we've inherited, gives literature a new definition and a new name. At the extreme, it only valorizes literature on the condition that it quits the physical space of assembly and encounter, which is doubly devalued: first, in an absolutist form proper to a royal court; second, as the transitional mode of the salons leading toward a veritable democratic public sphere. Literature's public becomes one of these abstractions, in relationship with that other abstraction that is the public-people of democracy. It finds its antimodel in the public of spectacles: corporeal, concrete, made up of individuals, often grumbling and bellowing, bad smelling, potentially dangerous. All our representation of literature, as a model of modern democracies, is founded upon this distinction. And so is modernity in its entirety.

Now, this model has been largely called into question, notably by feminist theory, and particularly by a text that is foundational for our epoch, "Rethinking the Public Sphere" by Nancy Fraser:

> The problem is not only that Habermas idealizes the liberal public sphere but also that he fails to examine other, nonliberal, non-bourgeois, competing public spheres.[25]

Fraser reminds us here that this idealized public sphere rests on a great many exclusions, the most important of which is gender, along with others based on class and racial criteria—inequalities of gender, class, and ethnicity. Significantly, Fraser points out that one of the things at stake in establishing the liberal public sphere was the elimination of the salons, that literary culture that was very strongly feminized, a literary culture that was the very paragon of a network system, opposing a community of readers to the brutish mob. One can therefore assume that the ideology of literature that excludes all practice *in praesentia* is indeed a corollary to the political ideology of the abstract unity of the public sphere. Fraser continues:

Virtually contemporaneous with the bourgeois public there arose a host of competing counterpublics, including national-ist publics, popular peasant publics, elite women's publics, and working class publics.[26]

However, according to the way Habermas reads modernity, and the way to which we have grown accustomed, these concurrent counterpublics, developing their own different comprehension of sharing a time, evidently did not exist—for the simple reason that the idealized public sphere was supposed to be welcoming everyone under the banner of the appearance of equality. But according to Fraser, that apparent equality did not exist. The ap-pearance of equality is a tool for getting the dominated to consent to new forms of inequality and new forms of consent, with the implication that

> the proliferation of a multiplicity of competing publics is neces-sarily a step away from, rather than toward, greater democracy, and that a single, comprehensive public sphere is always prefer-able to a nexus of multiple publics.[27]

Nancy Fraser's theory is exactly the inverse: she demonstrates how, in every type of society, the appearance of what she calls (following Spivak) "subaltern counterpublics" does indeed advance the society more toward the ideal of parity of participation in its debates and deliberations than the concept of a single public sphere. So we need to distinguish communities from publics, noting that publics are performative and temporary and that one can belong to different publics at the same time. With this political proposition, Fraser unites Spivak (and her idea of subaltern counterpublics) with Ju-dith Butler (and her idea of performativity), and this proposition is essential to contemporary worlds—from the political point of view and the cultural, and with regard to both subjectivities and collectives.

The idealization of the public sphere becomes valorized through silence, the opposite of brouhaha, and it situates itself in opposition to my propositions concerning the contemporary. One must maintain silence about real inequalities to achieve an equality in principle. Now, to return to viewing the idealized public sphere as a literary sphere, I emphasize that the idea of literature imposed during modernity was very strongly linked to silence and, again, very strongly opposed to brouhaha. Literary history tells us, for example, how the history of poetry is a story of gradual detachment from external music in favor of an interiorized music. It tells us how the ideal dramatic text abandons the theater in favor of the armchair, how the novel has no need to be read aloud, and that this is the reason it has come to dominate all the other genres. Not that the idealized public sphere condemns the "arts of spectacle," but on the contrary, they are disciplined through the idea of catharsis, that tool for regulating unruly passions. Literature is captured within the frame of silent communication *in absentia,* and therefore it cannot in any respect be spatial, nor public, nor oral.

Now, just as there are subaltern counterpublics opposed to the idealized public sphere, so there are subaltern counterpublics who oppose the ideal of a silent literature, who advance instead toward the counter-ideal model of brouhaha. These literary subaltern counterpublics are not necessarily the expression of "sociopolitical" subaltern counterpublics but are the expression of a literary practice that is not constructed upon the triple exclusion of space, body, and sound. A number of historical studies have shown how the two (counterpublics and nonexclusive literary practices) are often linked—notably, studies by Richard Hoggart in Great Britain, Jacques Rancière in France, and Lawrence Levine in the United States.[28] We read here how workers and "the poor" have historically tended toward a performative approach to literature. Many historical studies show how the literary ideal was hegemonic but not total. Poetic performances and public lectures have always accompanied the diffusion of written works, but they have been reduced to silence by the dominant historiography.

We could argue that these moments of inscription of the literary in public spaces (lectures, performances, exhibitions, etc.) arise out of a logic proper to subaltern counterpublics. The best proof, I believe, is in the reaction they often incite. Such forms are rejected as being not really literature but only noise or babbling and as being in some way communitarian. And yet, the reproach of communitarianism comes from those who have idealized the public sphere and do not want to recognize the fact that there are multitudes of public spaces, both temporary and coexisting.

THE CONTEMPORARY MOMENT OF LITERATURES

On the contrary, I argue that this multitude of public spaces constitutes the contemporary moment of literature, just as the public sphere of Literature characterized its modern representation. If these public spaces have always existed, even when they were silenced, they have never been more numerous or more visible than they are today. They have not only multiplied but greatly diversified, so widely that literature today appears in large part as if it were an arena of conflict between a hegemonic public sphere built on print publication and a multitude of counterhegemonic public spaces marked by "brouhaha literature"—literature exhibited, performed, on site, with multiple types of support—and with a great deal of circulation between the two.

We might legitimately hypothesize that the subaltern counterpublics, considering the triumph of Literature as linked to that of the male, Western bourgeois class, had to find a path for uniting the literary and the political within the forms of brouhaha-literature. This might account for the career of American singer Gil Scott-Heron, for example, who wrote two novels[29] before "inventing," in the early 1970s, that peculiar genre of poetry called "spoken word," in reaction to the failure of his fiction in the white New York publishing world, and in contrast to the impression the Last Poets made on him. We can see brouhaha-literature, then, as arising out of gender, class, and ethnic exclusions. The phenomenon is more than simply a convergence of struggles. It is the nonreproduction of the tools of domination that modernity had engendered. In this case, a certain number of literary traditions that were not part of Literature, traditions from the non-Western world, were given new life.

This suggests another kind of antihegemonic approach, internal to literature itself and based on the distinction between the publication of literature in book form and publication outside of that form—a distinction between traditional publication and new forms of making-public. While it would be difficult to generalize systematically about the global field of publishing, a few traits do stand out. Structurally speaking, the world publishing market shares the same characteristics as other ultracompetitive markets; that is, it employs the economic model of the "fringe oligopoly"[30] (in which production is increasingly concentrated in a few enormous international groups, accompanied by the obliteration of smaller, more restricted producers). This is true on the national scale as well as the international. Not only are all the mid-level publishers in the process of vanishing but so is the research side of the industry. The aesthetic effects of standardization are such that the publication of book-form literature increasingly poses real problems for its creators nowadays. And in fact, the symbolic capital of book-form publication is increasingly being questioned. A reading in a packed theater may have more value than a traditional publication.

This is especially true if we consider that the cultural swing toward social practices and the relational swing toward public politics, whether they arise from public or private sources, encourage a weeding out of new fields. There are many examples of this, examples that are both widely diverse and sometimes contradictory.

Today, practically any site devoted to exhibition has a cultural program aimed at what are henceforth called "publics." Rather than trying to reproduce the specificity of other sites, like movie theaters and concert halls, devoted to the diffusion of works to various publics, that cultural program opens itself up to other possibilities, including the open exploration of nonprinted literature. The phenomenon is massive; one of its most dramatic examples so far was the creation in 2013 of the post of "poet laureate" at MoMA. As its first laureate, the underground poet Kenneth Goldsmith began a series of performances titled "Guerilla Readings," inviting a group of authors, from Vanessa Place to Charles Bernstein, to participate in the insertion of literature into public spaces.

Another point, adding onto the previous: political publics have long relied on the idea of culture as a vector of social cohesion. In other times, this would entail a monumental, extravagant approach, supposedly creating meaning for the community. But today, this would be contrary to the newly privileged micropolitics, which favor the inclusion of artists—and why not writers as well?—into an existing social fabric. We can imagine residencies for writers, studios for writing, developing in an exponential manner and inscribing literary practice into social space.

A third example is the institutionalization of creative writing within the pedagogical framework of schools and universities. In such cases, the teacher-writer is paid less for what she or he publishes and more for what she or he teaches—and after all, if we're going to talk about symbolic capital, we shouldn't ignore economic capital. Within the framework of the fringe oligopoly, printed literature only rarely affords the author a living. Authors make their living (with some rare exceptions) from residencies, grants, and, above all, teaching, much more than from their actual books. According to one of the best commentators on this phenomenon, Mark McGurl,[31] we have the privilege of working at a historic moment within the reconfiguration of the literary field. What he calls the "program era" ("program" here being used in the sense of university creative writing programs) is a new model, conforming neither to the concept of heteronomy nor to that of autonomy, to use Pierre Bourdieu's terminology;[32] it is a model conforming neither to the premodern patronage framework nor to that of the modern economic one. Today, especially in the United States, a classically capitalist literary system coexists with another system, which developed within universities but which has grown to constitute the single most important literary development since the Second World War. This phenomenon, for better or worse, is founded upon the presence of literature in public spaces, in this case the sites of cultural transmission, where publication, or making-public, is always plural, books themselves being only a small part of it. In this system, brouhaha-literature has leaped ahead of Literature.

One final phenomenon: the realm of writing has never been so extensive, nor has the idea of publication ever been so plural. Not a day passes without a great percentage of humanity publishing one or numerous texts: on a blog, a social media network, or elsewhere. To publish no longer means to participate in that marvelous, abstract public sphere Habermas described. On the contrary, publishing or making public is now a matter of multiplying one's text within public spaces. We might point to the huge corpus of fanfiction: without entering into debate about its literary value, we can admire how it rests on publishing protocols both sophisticated and inventive, protocols that have allowed hundreds of thousands of people to participate in the field we call "writing."

On a much more artistic side, we could point to the fascinating project, developing in France over the last several years, under the title of *The Encyclopedia of Speech (Encyclopédie de la parole)*, describing itself thus:

> *The Encyclopedia of Speech* is a collective project seeking to understand transversally the diversity of oral forms.
> Since September of 2007, *The Encyclopedia of Speech* has

collected all sorts of records and has catalogued them according to the particular elements of the word: cadences, choral forms, compressions, emphases, spacings, melodies, repetitions, residue, saturations, timbers, etc. Each of these terms has an entry in the *Encyclopedia,* accompanied by an audio file and an explanatory notice.

From these records, *The Encyclopedia of Speech* produces sound files, shows, performances, seminars, installations, a game, all of which are presented at public openings.

The Encyclopedia of Speech is run by a collective of poets, plastic artists, musicians, curators, directors, dramaturges, choreographers, and radio producers. Its slogan is: "We are all speech experts."[33]

So what marks our time is the end of the representation of literature as being uniquely a printed object and part of the idealized public sphere. A different representation is coming into being: that of a more or less conflictual arena, in which the literature of that public sphere enters into dialogue with the brouhaha-literature of a multitude of public spaces. Henceforth Literature is only one of the possible actualizations of literature and of publication. To repeat: there is no substitution, only addition.

These three examples do not exhaust the profound mutations taking place across literature over the last thirty years, which are forcing us to alter our imaginary. The image of the solitary author speaking through his book *in absentia* and addressing a mass, anonymous audience—this was the image that functioned in the idealized public sphere, the model of modern democracies, but it corresponds only very partially to the reality of literature today.

It does not correspond to the multiple literary practices that have been developing at an exponential rate, engaging not only new aesthetics but also a new economy not based solely on authors' rights and book sales. It does not correspond to the new social aspect of literature, based on visibility. From bookstore signings to public readings to the development of huge festivals, we are witnessing a transformation in the social presence of the author. The old model does not correspond to the massive introduction of contemporary literature in the schools and universities, reconfiguring the spaces, objectives, and methods of recognition. It does not correspond to the upheaval of the cultural economy brought about by the digital revolution, which has upended the long-standing circuit of author to reader, mediated by the publisher; that circuit was incarnated in an object, the book, and produced a certain idea of literature. It no longer corresponds to the technical conditions of textual production (such as computer-based typesetting), which have unified the tools of production, publication, distribution, and reception, making once-firm borders between those domains entirely porous. It does not correspond to contemporary mediatized culture, which no longer separates and distinguishes high art on one side and cultural practices on the other. The literary is thus conceived less and less as a kind of exception among other exceptions, such as the artistic and religious, and is now seen as one kind of social communication within a large ensemble of kinds of social communication. It does not correspond to the last half-century's extraordinary burst of mass marketing and diversification, which no longer relies upon an imaginary of rarity. Finally, it corresponds less and less to the hegemonic Euro-American model but instead takes account of the diversity of representations and the multiple translational channels opened up by globalization and minority counterwriting.

If there's one thing these transformations have in common, it's that they're all moving from a representation and thus an imaginary of the literary centered on a support object (the book) to an imaginary of the literary centered on an action and a practice: publication. Publication, however, has returned to its original sense, making public; it no longer denotes a private expression aimed at precise correspondents but rather one aimed at more and more diverse publics. The publication of literature is not historically limited to that of books. The publics of literature have never been limited to readers. There are as many literatures as possibilities of publication: books, performances, readings, salons, groups, diverse digital spaces. Each of these literatures creates its own specific public space. Moreover, this new era of publication overflows the frame of literature. Exhibition and performance (in the visual and dramatic arts) are in this sense specific modes of publication, which then become the grand transversal, interdisciplinary concept allowing us to imagine artistic and cultural expressions rather than works of art. And beyond artistic practices, the concept of publication has political implications. Jürgen Habermas made literary communication via the book into the idealized model of a democratic society on the march toward rationality, but it is necessary to ask ourselves what political imaginary produces the pluralization of the idea of publication. And finally, if we take account of the many ongoing debates concerning confidentiality and privacy in the information society, we can conclude that publication is one of the key concepts of the contemporary.

TOWARD AN IMAGINARY OF PUBLICATION

Our investigation of the literary world took Agamben's celebrated seminar lecture as its point of departure. It was centered on the literary, not through some personal predilection of mine (though that is real enough) but because the theories concerning the sharing of a time and the forms of communities that they produce are based on two centuries of literary imaginaries. "Literature," that is, sacralized literature, arises out of a specifically modern imaginary, but it also profoundly structures the modern experience of the world. That experience rests fundamentally on the practice of a silent reading producing an abstract and idealized community, which itself arises from an abstract and idealized community. This community, in the view of Habermas, is a "good" community, the model of a rational and consensual society. But in reality, it is exclusionary and segregationist.

This model, so powerful that it was able to establish an order of knowing and embed it in the university, can withstand neither a historical examination nor observation from the present day. On one hand, as Nancy Fraser has shown, although this model was hegemonic in Europe and the United States, it was not total. Likewise, other models have continued to proliferate and evolve, valorizing brouhaha-literature and the constitution of minority publics (not just a white, male, bourgeois community) through a practice of performance literature. And it's also true that the hegemonic model was only in place for two centuries, and only in a small (although very powerful) part of the world. Finally, the contemporary experience of literature continues to multiply itself, to contextualize itself, and to favor oral, performed, exhibited literatures, and so well that the literary imaginary of the contemporary is much more the expression of a multiplicity of publics and counterpublics than of a unique community. We must also add that the literary idealization of the human community is fragile in a world where literature itself no longer occupies the central position that it once did—a position that in fact was sometimes uncertain. Given that fact, it is no longer so certain that the literary imaginary established community imaginaries. But the fact that literature no longer occupies the center does not mean that literary experience (an enlarged literary experience) must be in trouble. On the contrary: literature and the practice of publication have never been so diffuse, multiple, and diverse. But they are all integrated within the imaginary of publication. In my view, this is the problem posed by Giorgio Agamben's text and the reading that it is usually given. It rests upon an imaginary of Literature that is segregationist and separating, an imaginary that the contemporary has put into crisis.

FOURTH SERIES

Controversy

BUT WHAT ABOUT POSTMODERNISM?
CIRCA 1960–1990: THE EMPIRE

Our inquiry has already introduced us to many of the worlds of the contemporary. Only traces remain from Rosario. On the Internet, you can still find the texts from the Centro de Expresiones Contemporáneas under the rubric "¿Qué es lo contemporáneo?" And if you're patient enough, you can even find some images from the publication—which sometimes appears as a whole, sometimes in part, and is often projected for a future date. On the blogs, launch parties for forthcoming issues are discussed more than the actual publications themselves—not surprising for a series interested in the public space of art. As for the Rouen moment, our goal was to draw out the architectural modern–postmodern paradigm by reflecting on the epoch and the mediatization the times imposed upon it. These two first substantivations of the contemporary preceded the (very refined) totemic magnum opus on the contemporary, that of Giorgio Agamben, who opened up the third of the worlds we explored. It led us to a political understanding of the modern community, founded by the literary imaginary—an imaginary thrown into crisis by the contemporary. This was also revealed in the Pantin project that, with its three components, distanced itself from the literary imaginary of modernity and instead inscribed itself in that of publication. Meanwhile, at the beginning of our second series, we missed an opportunity to examine the postmodern—a word that comes up often, not to say incessantly, in discussions of the contemporary.

So we now need to take a moment to reflect on this term, since I didn't want to do so at that earlier point. I didn't want our inquiry to follow a kind of preordained logical sequence—modern, postmodern, contemporary. Ideas don't evolve like that. But the method we've been using, retracing the manner in which concepts come to be questioned, can be used again for the postmodern, since it was the object of two parallel and conflictual questions that tell us a lot about the fleeting brilliance of its existence. The first, triumphant but already ironic, reuses the formula Kant used with the Enlightenment: "Response to the Question: What Is the Postmodern?"[1] locates the postmodern as succeeding the Enlightenment. The second, melancholic and bewildered, asks, "What Happened to the Postmodern?" The author of this question answered it by saying, "Not very much, though it seemed like such a good idea."[2]

In the history of recent debates, the dispute over the postmodern is not a trivial one, especially when we consider the principal actors. It is worthwhile to recall the conditions of our investigation into the substantivation of *contemporary*. The two substantivations are in a chiasmus-like relation to each other: one is spectacular but without any lasting impact; the other is more understated but foundational. Putting these two in opposition with each other serves no purpose, for they are inscribed within the same movement. Let's return to the spectacular aspect of the debate. It's enough, for example, to recall what may be called the highest point of the debate: the dispute between Jean-François Lyotard and Jürgen Habermas, which Richard Rorty attempted to moderate, but which ended with the domination of Fredric Jameson. Observing the conditions of the debate some thirty years later, it's easy to see that this was a debate carried out by a set of old white men, philosophers, all over the age of fifty (born between 1924 and 1934), European and American, or more specifically, men who came from the three points that sought to dominate the intellectual and artistic space of the world in the early 1980s: France, Germany, the United States. These men were not just anybody—in the animal world, they would be called alpha males—and their books are fundamental ones in the international intellectual world. It's not surprising that the one who ended up carrying the day was the newcomer, Fredric Jameson.

I should make it very clear so as not to be misunderstood: I have a deep respect for these thinkers, whose work is and has been a major theoretical contribution, a respect that I hope is recognizable throughout certain pages of this book. None of them would have wanted to be described, thirty years later, as a dominant white male. The nature of their dispute is what makes it seem that way, because that dispute was being quietly undermined from all sides by the brouhaha contemporary with it: Donna Haraway's "A Cyborg Manifesto" (1985);[3] Spivak's "subalterns"[4] (1988); Ngugi wah Thiong'o's "decolonization of the mind" (1986);[5] Appiah's[6] and Shohat's[7] reflections on "post-" (1991 and 1992, respectively). In these other books, we find the dynamic that is at work throughout this essay. A linear and sequential majority movement was unaware of the turbulences surrounding it—though, in this case, it was those turbulences that were going to become far more important. The reconstitution of the historical postmodern has until recently only been a matter of a "great" debate among dominant white males. The marker *post-* only designates an epoch; it is a weak marker, formed out of a simple modulation of the contents of modernity, while other far more substantial and amodern concepts were being developed. Today, these are the concepts that matter. But for a long time, and still today to some extent, some have wanted to situate us within the trope of an aftertime. I want to turn now to a reexamination of that dispute and the brouhaha that accompanied it. This reexamination will be, like the other sites in our inquiry, a case study, in fact a study of the debates that have shaped our present.

I will not trace the history of postmodernity—Perry Anderson has already done an admirable job of that in his *Origins of Postmodernity*;[8] instead, I will simply point out that the word's meanings are multiple and sometimes contradictory, just like that prefix *post-* that encumbers it and implies both rupture and continuity, beginning and ending, achievement and decline. I will also point out that this prefix *post-* has been used with a series of names, beginning to multiply in the 1960s, denoting historical and social mutations.

It is quite striking that most of the analyses of these mutations scarcely touch upon what seems essential to us today—that is, as we noted earlier, the demographic and sociological changes following the war, notably the spread in Europe and North America of democratization and of newly opened access to knowledge, culture, and creativity for the masses. This movement has been so powerful that it is comparable to the spread of literacy that accompanied modernity in Europe. A new generation, an extremely large one owing to the demographic boom that followed World War II, was abruptly granted access to educational institutions at all levels and to the sites of social and cultural promotion and distinction. This generation broke the cycle that had been put in place for so long, in which each new generation saw its sons and daughters as having the same sociocultural horizon as their fathers and mothers. And it also broke a connection to tradition. In any case, the apparatuses of reception—schools, universities, museums, concert halls—could not be content simply to expand in order to welcome these new publics. They underwent profound changes, rethinking their own relation to historical processes. It was, clearly, a matter of these newcomers carrying out a symbolic killing of the father. The destruction of sculptures used as teaching materials for French art schools is one of the most legendary images. This vandalism meant that the process of transmission had to change.

It had to be less founded on tradition, erudition, and virtuosity and much more on the present. This entailed a different relation to historical time and altered social and cultural practices, changes that the word *postmodern* was to describe (for that generation). A new tradition had to be invented, a new objective (for the schools and artistic institutions helping to situate the student or citizen in the contemporary world, as reflected in school curricula), and new methods. And they all had to be invented starting from that which forms the specificity of this generation: to be alive.[9]

For we must not forget that the current generation is moving, more rapidly than any other and in large numbers, into the offices, onto the podiums, and into the sites of decision making, and that this movement is in turn renewing the principles of the same process of the democratization of access to knowledge and culture. For such a renewal to succeed, a generation needs to dedicate itself to the task, and to do that, it needs to find a way to distinguish itself as different. This is the role the word *postmodern* played as a differential marker, and it's the same role that the word *contemporary* has played for some twenty years now. For just as with all such names, it, too, required a struggle and a seizing of power. The aesthetic analyses of such tipping-point moments are too often concerned with the consequences and not enough with the structural causes. For example, the distinction between "high" and "low" culture is often presented as symbolic of the postwar cultural changes, whereas in fact it's only an offshoot of that specific era of democratization and of opening up access to culture and knowledge to the masses.

But the story of postmodernity usually omits any mention of those changes. The postmodern was first conceptualized in the fields of literary theory and architecture,[10] but the meanings assigned to it in those two cases were quite different. On the literary side, it was a matter of an ultramodernity, an intensified modern with some new characteristics, notably a new interest in popular cultures. On the architectural side, it was instead a kind of anti-modernity, assuming the form of a return to the decorative instead of the functional. But what they most had in common was illustrating how postmodernity was much more an American story, or rather a story about the United States seemingly taking up a position of dominance over the chief issues of modernity. And in this regard, we should note how the debate involving Lyotard, Habermas, and Rorty also bore witness to the struggle between the United States and Europe for artistic and intellectual hegemony in a world where the "cultural" had come to take on considerable importance. No matter the angle from which one approaches postmodernism, whether from the angle of the counterculture (where it presents itself as an alliance between intellectual and popular cultures, political activism and hedonism) or from the opposite side, from that of conservatism (where postmodernism is presented as a reaction against the "excesses" of modernity, a reaction sometimes seemingly neoclassical, sometimes simply kitsch), one has to say, for better or for worse, that postmodernism was an American passion, nourished by these models.

But during the second moment of problematizing the postmodern, the moment of the debate among the Franco–Germanic–American thinkers, we see the intellectual authorities putting the postmodern into order, taming what had escaped them and what had in fact brought them together. This *putting into order* meant the end of the brouhaha and the beginning of a traditional debate. Without sounding too much like an extreme formalist, I will note that the form of the debate is more important than its content for understanding a concept's historical mutations. For example, modernity is characterized by a taming of brouhaha by the authorities. The contemporary is characterized by the impossibility of this kind of attempt at a domestication. The debate over the postmodern is a paradigmatic example.

The main themes of the story are familiar. There can be no

great theory of historical time, or of the present, or of the epochal without the apparatus of a modern validation: a book by a single author, likely to be a philosopher, that supposedly "sheds light on a dark present moment" (already we feel the presence of Agamben's thesis). But neither Jencks, nor Venturi, nor Hassan could shoulder this task. Jean-François Lyotard could, and he did so with his *The Postmodern Condition*—a strange book, to be honest, announcing at the outset that it is a "report on the condition of knowledge in the most highly developed societies." Its principal mantra is still often invoked: the end of "metanarratives," the end of the grand narratives, the narratives of legitimation that allow one to say that a law is just and a statement is true. Such narratives, for Lyotard, are specifically modern. They allow for all fields of knowledge to be brought together around a fable that legitimates them, which in turn legitimates the fable. Such, for example, are "the dialectics of Spirit, the hermeneutics of meaning, the emancipation of the rational or working subject, the creation of wealth" or the classless society.[11] "This is the Enlightenment narrative, in which the hero of knowledge works toward a good ethico-political end, universal peace." Opposing such narratives, Lyotard evokes the development of concurrent "small narratives," always already there but always about to be performed. The postmodern condition, thus, is a transitory, performative, dissensual condition, one that does not seek out resolution. "Invention," Lyotard writes, "is always born of dissension,"[12] another term from the lexicon of brouhaha. Or better, "consensus is only a particular state of discussion, not its end."[13] Lyotard's book is often caricatured and simplified. For example, so many *stories* about the epoch have been written using this mantra about the end of metanarratives, producing an endless metanarrative of their end without ever opening themselves up to the real multiplicity of minor narratives—without allowing them to be heard, without attending to them, without accepting their possible resolution. The book, even though its author later

referred to it as "very bad," is nonetheless very important. Without falling into the opposite kind of caricature, one could call it
visionary, because it was one of the first works to link knowledge,
processes of legitimation, institutions, and the structures of social ties with narratives or fables. Lyotard's book was one of the
first to reveal modernity's essential condition of narrative and to
describe modernity as a narrative with a unifying vocation; *The
Postmodern Condition* was one of the first works to consider the
agonistic pluralization of legitimation processes, one of the first to
consider the contemporary as brouhaha. Written early in the era
of the information society, the book is still capable of surprising
us when we see it already examining information as a commodity
and, above all, as a control apparatus.

Strangely, amid a near-total misunderstanding, it produced
almost the inverse of what it announced. It almost invited the
legitimated savants to come and debate, with all their authority,
the postmodern condition. Jürgen Habermas was taken to task in
Lyotard's book as one who had sought to orient "our treatment of
the problem of legitimation in the direction of a search for universal
consensus through what he calls *Diskurs,* in other words, a dialogue
of argumentation."[14] Habermas's response was not slow in coming. It took the form of an "anti-postmodern" lecture, translated
in the journal *Critique* in 1981 under the title of "Modernity: An
Unfinished Project." Lyotard replied in the same journal, using a
title that brings us back to the beginning of the book, and to the
questioning method upon which my own inquiry rests: "Response
to the Question: What is the Postmodern?" After the French philosopher, and then the German philosopher, it seemed logical for
an American philosopher to stride into the trans-Atlantic arena.
And so we witnessed two American philosophers enter into the
debate at the same time, in the spring of 1984: Richard Rorty—
although in a very civil way, too civil to be effective; and Fredric
Jameson, less well known at that time, with his seminal essay that

appeared in the *New Left Review*: "Postmodernism, or the Cultural Logic of Late Capitalism." Jameson produced what the others had been unable to do, a systematization, "an incomparably richer and more comprehensive mural of the age than any other record of this culture."[15] Jameson used the same title a few years later for a book that developed the ideas proposed in the 1984 article.

According to Perry Anderson, Jameson effected five major displacements in our understanding of the postmodern. Inspired by Ernest Mandel's theory of economic cycles, he saw in postmodernism a new cycle of capitalism, multinational in scope, in which culture and economy became one. The second displacement took place at the level of subjectivities, marked henceforth by an absence of depth. But it was perhaps on the subject of culture that Jameson's article and book have been the most influential. The panoramic ambition is stunning: from architecture to video, from literature to cinema and theory, from high-brow cultures to popular cultures, we witness an enormous despecialization of both practices and discourses, bringing everything together into one huge field, henceforth called "culture." After economy, psychology, culture, came the fourth displacement: all these become interconnected, concerning social organization on a global scale. Though class-based society had not disappeared, it had been transformed with new entities, centered on a set of superior classes surrounded by a whole complex of "segmented identities and localized groups, typically based on ethnic or sexual differences."[16] This new social organization was accompanied by the "integration of the entire planet into a global market." This system, hegemonic on a global scale, is for the first time the expression of a "specifically North American global style."[17] In my view, this is still the best definition: postmodernism portrays an American moment in history, which is not at all the same as the contemporary. If I wanted to be provocative, I could say that postmodernism is the seizing of power by dominant white males (regardless of their nationalities) within American institutions from dominant white males within European institutions. Anderson notes one final displacement. Jameson as theorist or critic does not pretend to be an outside observer separate from a fragmented postmodernity; rather, he presents himself as an actor implicated within a postmodernity conceived of as a system—which may, in fact, be the greatest contribution the book makes to the theory of the contemporary.

Fredric Jameson's article and book belong to that rare category of monument-books that are able to encompass the entirety of an epoch within a system. And even more remarkably, the epoch in question is his own. How then should we understand the fact that the book signals the disappearance of the category of postmodern rather than inaugurating a mass use of it?

CYBORGS AND SUBALTERNS

The answer to the question lies precisely in the fact that it was a monument-book, able to encompass the entirety of an epoch within a system. Because it's a great modernist book on the postmodern, pitting the "great intellectual," all alone, up against a titanic task. And maybe because the France–Germany–United States triangle was still in control after the article appeared but had become much less important by the time the book came out. Maybe because *post-*, or maybe because *modern*. Maybe because to name is to desire. And the potential of desire conveyed by the *after* is real but cannot be inscribed within the moment. I can think of yet another reason. It might be that, in hindsight, people misunderstood the book, notably because they mistook the context that shaped it. Again, narratives from hindsight warp our vision. They reorder things, eliminating anything that would disturb that order.

In 1984, Jameson may not have caused much concern to Lyotard, Habermas, or Rorty, but his seminal text can be connected to another set of books, much more important although less spectacular, about the substantivation of the contemporary. In fact, when he wrote this book, Jameson was a professor in the Department of History of Consciousness at the University of California at Santa Cruz. This department symbolizes and concretizes many of the aspects that we have been exploring and that we will continue to explore. In the short space of a dozen years, it brought together all of those thinkers who were going to go beyond and condemn the notion of the postmodern: the anthropologist James Clifford, the historian Hayden White, the comparatist Gayatri Chakravorty Spivak, the feminists Donna Haraway and Teresa de Lauretis, the activist Angela Davis, and, of course, Fredric Jameson. It was in the brouhaha of this department that the meanings of the contemporary were constructed, rather than in the *ex cathedra* pronouncements (made for those capable of "piercing the obscurity") about the meaning of the epoch. The contemporary is a collective, turbulent, fragmented, and sometimes contradictory construction. It bears no resemblance to the analyses offered by those I have called "dominant white males." This is why the fabric of the contemporary in the 1980s can be glimpsed microscopically in this university department, where texts that would be influential in the long term were conceived, texts that were to be even more influential than Jameson's. Texts that have bit by bit abandoned all reference to the postmodern, and even all reference to *post-*.

I am thinking specifically of two texts that mark a fundamental theoretical and intellectual turning point—two texts that are nearly the opposite of those, written at the very same time, that shaped the debate on postmodernism. They are Donna Haraway's "A Cyborg Manifesto" (1985)[18] and Gayatri Spivak's *Can the Subaltern Speak?* (1988).[19] Before discussing what these books say, let's pause to consider what they *did*. Their greatest contribution was perhaps to think through the conditions of speaking (something the debate on postmodernism never did). And they showed that the usage of speech had been colonized by a vision of history and of the present, above all that of modern emancipation, and that decolonization was urgently needed. They offered, therefore, not only content but a method and a politics.

Donna Haraway foregrounds her links with the university at Santa Cruz by speaking of her manifesto as a collective text. The conditions of speaking have radically changed. This is an almost collective text, not a monument to an individual's prowess—a manifesto, constantly revised, never frozen in one state, bringing together professors and students, citing both in an egalitarian and indivisible manner. This is not a matter of dialogue carried on in the highest spheres but rather a matter of connecting different acts of speech. Among them is Jameson on postmodernism, which here takes on a very different meaning. Donna Haraway includes herself in the group of postmodern theorists; she does so implicitly or explicitly when she calls her text "an attempt to contribute to feminist socialist culture and theory in a postmodern mode." The terms "postmodern," "postmodernist," and "postmodernism" recur often in the manifesto, but their conceptualization is never truly fixed. Jameson's article is very present both in the manifesto and in its notes, but it is always being surpassed or, rather, used toward other ends. And "A Cyborg Manifesto" is, politically, a great deal clearer than the postmodernist theories that it uses, notably in the way it proposes to reread modernity:

> In the traditions of "Western" science and politics—the tradition of racist male-dominant capitalism; the tradition of progress; the tradition of the appropriation of natural resources for the productions of culture; the tradition of reproducing the self from the reflections of the other—the relation between organism and machine has been a border war. The stakes in the border war have been the territories of production, reproduction, and imagination. This chapter is an argument for pleasure in the confusion of boundaries and for responsibility in their construction.[20]

When we recall the discussion of Jauss and Latour in our introduction, this extract is striking, for it combines almost all the issues, opposing itself to borders, advocating confusion and denouncing the modern narrative. It is also exciting to see how Haraway's text goes beyond, displaces, outpaces the terms of the debate between Lyotard and Habermas (while remaining much closer to Lyotard). For it is a matter of bringing out the distinction between History and histories, between History and Narratives, but in order to replace them with an eminently political, altogether new framework. From one angle, consider this holy trinity:

> The West and its most important corollary, the preponderance of the one that is neither animal, nor barbarian, nor woman: man, author of a cosmos called History.[21]

From another, histories in the plural, conceived as "tools":

> Stories retold, new versions that overturn and displace the hierarchical dualisms that organize the identities constructed on a so-called nature.[22]

Her program resonates well with the pluralization of public spaces, dehierarchization, and the structures we have been exploring from the outset.

On the one hand, we are a long way from the debate within Western modernity that Lyotard and Habermas represented; on the other, we are even further from the relatively sterile debates that followed regarding the distinction between grand narratives or metanarratives and small or minor narratives. History from this point onward is a political site; the very ideas of speech and writing are being reinvented. With History, speech and writing have been stolen, pillaged, colonized, and this in two senses: first, because they have been associated with Western phallogocentrism, and second, because this same Western phallogocentrism has taught us a history that defines excluded populations as deprived of their own speech and writing (this can include both the mass of humans and nonhuman environments of Bruno Latour[23]). So "A Cyborg Manifesto" does battle with a double silencing. This is why "contests for the meanings of writing are a major form of contemporary political struggle."[24] It is also why Haraway presents cyborg politics in this way:

> Writing is pre-eminently the technology of cyborgs, etched surfaces of the late twentieth century. Cyborg politics is the struggle for language and the struggle against perfect communication, against the one code that translates all meaning perfectly, the central dogma of phallogocentrism. That is why cyborg politics insists on noise and advocates pollution, rejoicing in the illegitimate fusions of animal and machine.[25]

At last, here we are: noise, pollution, brouhaha. "A Cyborg Manifesto" makes a profound change in the situation, setting out the definitional traits of the contemporary that my study has been drawing out from the beginning. In the struggles to define the present, the cursor moves content into positions of enunciation, into speech acts, into legitimacies. This is not in any sense a formalism. With any statement, no matter what kind, we must always ask who is speaking, with what authority, and making what use of speech, for the first exclusions are the ones that matter most for the discourse. Haraway tells us, among other more specific propositions, that the contemporary epoch will be one of unveiling, of the deconstruction of coherent and naturalized narratives, products of a modernity constructed upon the trinity West–Man–History. We are no longer in a kind of after-time, in a kind of soft negativity, but in the company of a highly positive method, one that, thirty years later, we now recognize as inaugural. Brouhaha thus becomes both the site and the apparatus of the contemporary.

We must also mention a third text fundamental to contemporary theory and to the theory of the contemporary that emerged from the "Santa Cruz moment": "Can the Subaltern Speak?" Spivak's theoretical and political gesture is a very violent one, with a violence directed not toward her apparent enemies but instead toward those who, at first glance, would appear to be allies: those whom she calls "French intellectuals," who, as it turns out, are named Gilles Deleuze and Michel Foucault, "our best prophets of heterogeneity and the Other,"[26] but who, despite their most laudable efforts, are ultimately not free of the West–Man–History trinity; they have never freed themselves from the contradictions of modernity and postmodernity. Another major actor in the theory wave of the early 1980s had just made a similar gesture: Edward Said. In his book *Orientalism*,[27] Said made a point of keeping his distance from Michel Foucault. But Spivak's critique with regard to Foucault remains the weightiest in terms of its consequences, for, in her view, Foucault constructed solid theoretical representations of politics but never articulated them with good aims, or rather with good methods, blinded as he was by imperialist thinking. Spivak's text (and this is a point of some significance) largely comprises commentary not on a book, nor even on an article, but on an interview that appeared in the newspapers between Deleuze and Foucault, "because it undoes the opposition between authoritative theoretical production and the unguarded practice of conversation."[28] According to her, this allows us to see the "mark of ideology" more clearly, but one can also see in it a valorization of speech and noise versus the order and discipline of an authorized text. For the stakes are always the same—that is, speech: who is speaking? In whose name? Now, for Spivak, the question is settled: "the Other as subject is inaccessible for Foucault and Deleuze."[29] They are incapable of taking account of the "muted subject of the female subaltern."

Spivak's text is highly tactical, attempting to effect a displacement within the field of critique itself. Whereas one might think that Foucault and Deleuze would lead us to the point where the oppressed could finally, not simply speak—because they have never ceased speaking—*but be heard,* to the point where the intellectual's duty would be to provide a forum for what up until now had been silenced, Spivak attempts to show how the approaches of Foucault and Deleuze remain trapped within the representation of a unique subject, the masses, the people, women, and how their approach turns out to be deceptive, leading us back into the imperialism of the sovereign subject. One might bypass the whole theoretical framework and go down the slope of artistic representations, for this debate is one of the period's most bitter.

Creating a space so that unheard voices can be heard, so that unseen bodies can be seen—this would appear to be one of the orders of the day in literature, cinema, and contemporary art, especially in documentary forms, which are enjoying an unheard-of expansion in terms of production, theoretical and critical investment, and recognition.[30] So much so that the documentary form is one of those that most surely signal the contemporary epoch. But Spivak's text tends to relativize the promises of emancipation that this aesthetic assumes.

This is because, in her view, the subaltern woman is always caught between two phrases that speak for her:

> One never encounters the testimony of women's voice-consciousness.[31]

She uses the example of the immolation-suicide of widows in India, reduced to silence by the two discourses that speak for them: "White men save brown women from brown men" or "The women wanted to die." The postcolonial intellectual, confronted with these phrases, "asks the question of simple semiosis—What does this signify?—and begins to plot a history."[32] And if "the origin of [her] sentence is thus lost in the shuffle between other, more powerful discourses,"[33] the only question that can attain such a power in the contemporary epoch is, Can the subaltern speak? It is she, woven into a history, who imposes a reconfiguration of knowledge, a transfer from philosophy to an extended theory of literature, from the Western intellectual to the postcolonial intellectual, from critical transparency to *positionality.*

So we can no longer say, "It doesn't matter who's speaking." We might even affirm the inverse: from now on, "it always matters who's speaking." The former assertion, according to Spivak, arises out of the modern European and U.S. intellectual structure and eventually out of its postmodern prolongation. That indifference to the speaking subject returns us, in her view, to an imperialist sovereignty. Her short text also takes us from one *post-* to another: from postmodernism (entirely devoid of any thought that would give the concept value) to postcolonialism. The postcolonial is presented as adversarial to the modern and the postmodern. Spivak's text is absolutely seminal, not only for what it says but also for where it leads us: to insist on the positionality of the theoretician, to displace the classic strategic alliances, to slip from one *post-* (postmodern) representing the old imperialist guard to another *post-* (postcolonial) that structures the contemporary—this is to construct a new sequence "provincializing" Europe, to adapt the polemical title of a book by Dipesh Chakrabarty.[34]

So, this question of the *post-*: is it settled once and for all? Of course not, because postmodernism and postcolonialism, so violently opposed in the texts we have been discussing, are nevertheless constructed from the same basis. Moreover, that prefix is a temporal one and, for that reason alone, bases the idea within the homogeneity of the epoch. Another work situated within the series we have been tracing has become one of the monumental books of contemporary theoretical production—*The Location of Culture* by Homi Bhabha, in fact, opts to begin with the problem in its opening paragraph:

It is the trope of our times to locate the question of culture in the realm of the *beyond*. At the century's edge, we are less exercised by annihilation—the death of the author—or epiphany—the birth of the subject. Our existence today is marked by a tenebrous sense of survival, living on the borderlines of the "present," for which there seems to be no proper name other than the current and controversial shiftiness of the prefix "post": postmodernism, postcolonialism, postfeminism.[35]

But Bhabha quickly turns to deconstruct the homogeneity of the epoch presupposed by the prefix *post-* and more subtly to reattack postmodernism in order to differentiate it from postcolonialism and postfeminism:

If the jargon of our times—postmodernity, postcolonialism, postfeminism—has any meaning at all, it does not lie in the popular use of the "post" to indicate sequentiality—*after* feminism—or polarity—*anti*-modernism. These terms that insistently gesture to the beyond only embody its restless and revisionary energy if they transform the present into an expanded and ex-centric site of experience and empowerment. For instance, if the interest in postmodernism is limited to a celebration of the fragmentation of the "grand narratives" of post-enlightenment rationalism then, for all its intellectual excitement, it remains a profoundly parochial enterprise.[36]

It would be wrong, then, to try to subsume under one referent, the *post-*, realities that can appear to be contradictory. On the contrary, Bhabha's text opens with a movement that other theoreticians of the contemporary have taken up as well: a movement to separate these different *posts* and a movement to deconstruct the *post* as a historical marker. These different *posts,* whatever their individual qualities, in one way or another lead us back to the centrality of the modern narrative. Now, it is precisely the deconstruction of the modern narrative, and above all its designation as a narrative, that signals the contemporary period. Must it be marked by tropes indicating an after, a survival, a beyond? And by all those sentiments that go along with them, especially a kind of melancholy?

No—provided we note that, as we have already seen and will continue to see, this deconstruction is based in modern sequentiality and that this *post* marks a problem in temporality. A problem we can dispense with by abandoning the use of it.

WE HAVE NEVER BEEN POSTMODERN

From Haraway to Spivak and Bhabha, we find in the critique of the modern and the postmodern that the latter is only conceived of as a prolongation of the former. We also find the same distrust with regard to using the *post* as a historical marker. It increasingly comes to appear as it really is, that is, as a simple syndrome, that of a crisis of time or rather as a crisis of temporality, and more precisely, a crisis of modern temporality. But a symptom that remains a prisoner to the concept that it designates. To understand this, one need only return to this essay's introduction. Thinking with the *post* is thinking like a modern, that is, thinking of time as a succession, with befores and afters, with sequences, with ruptures and borderlines. To be postmodern is only to be a modern who is tired of calling himself that. And of course, this is more or less the way Bruno Latour presented postmodernism in *We Have Never Been Modern*:

> for the moderns—as for their antimodern enemies, as well as for their false postmodern enemies—time's arrow is unambiguous.[37]

Postmodernism, nonetheless, remains interesting as a symptom. It can be seen as an intermediary phase. It has doubts about the modern temporal representation while at the same time being inscribed after it, like a kind of ending. Intellectually, this doesn't work. However, from the aesthetic point of view, for example, postmodernism, with its collages, its assemblages, its mashups, its impurity, is not without interest, but it is always situated in a dialectic with the modern, to which it plays the role of the "after." It would be difficult to put it any better than Latour does:

> The postmoderns retain the modern framework but disperse the elements that the modernizers grouped together in a well-ordered cluster. The postmoderns are right about the dispersion; every contemporary assembly is polytemporal. But they are wrong to retain the framework and to keep on believing in the requirement of continual novelty that modernism demanded. By mixing elements of the past together in collages and citations, the postmoderns recognize to what extent these citations are truly outdated. Moreover, it is because they are outmoded that the postmoderns dig them up, in order to shock the former "modernist" avant-gardes who no longer know at what altar to worship. But it is a long way from a provocative quotation extracted out of a truly finished past to a reprise, repetition or revisiting of a past that has never disappeared.[38]

The postmodern hypothesis appears now as an original weakness with regard to the modern hypothesis. On one hand, it retains its theoretical framework, but on the other, it loses all its power and homogeneity. For example, in squandering the possibility of a future, it breaks with the promises of modernity, even while reproducing its schema:

> Modernization was ruthless toward the premoderns, but what can we say about postmodernization? Imperialist violence at least offered a future, but sudden weakness on the part of the conquerors is far worse for, always cut off from the past, it now also breaks with the future. Having been slapped in the face with modern reality, poor populations now have to submit to postmodern hyperreality.[39]

Still, one can retain a certain fondness for the postmodern, especially in its antimodern conservatism, but it is a fondness for an intellectual attempt that is doomed to failure. And one can feel fond of it also because, within the history we have been documenting in this series, we can clearly view the dynamic that gave birth to postmodernism. This dynamic of doubting modernity, of doubting that singular temporality that irrevocably erased the past by means of a series of revolutions—those doubts allowed the emergence, under certain conditions, of that "Middle Kingdom, as vast as China and as little known,"[40] that is the contemporary conception of time. In this series, we can observe, running from Lyotard to Jameson, from Haraway to Spivak, and from Bhabha to Latour, something coming into view: the abandonment of the modern hypothesis, which the symptom of postmodernity helpfully allowed us to see.

NEITHER *POST-* NOR *ALTER-*, OR ENOUGH WITH THE PREFIXES

I cannot conclude this fourth series on controversy without mentioning another intermediary solution that has attracted considerable attention (in the realms of theory, politics, and media, including mass media) but that has run its course even more swiftly than the postmodern. Certainly this was a solution that appeared to dispense with sequentiality; certainly the semantic difficulty of the *post* did not weigh it down; certainly it had not withdrawn entirely into the realms of theory; but it was, nonetheless, a solution achieved by prefix—that is, a proposition that involved modulating something prior to itself. This solution substituted the prefix *alter-* for *post-* to form words like *altermodernity, altermodern*. It comes from the political arena, in fact from the militant political arena, unlike *postmodern,* which was in large part disconnected from politics. It then became disseminated within the art world, the inverse of postmodernism. Originating in extra-European struggles for the larger world's attention, it inscribed itself as a powerful articulation between the ideas of planetarity and historicity, because alter-modernity is founded on alterglobalization. For Michael Hardt and Antonio Negri, whose books have become international manu-als of such movements, altermodernity is born of antimodernity because it "traces," they say, "a decisive break with modernity and the power relations that define it," and it moves "from resistance to the proposition of alternatives."[41] Hardt and Negri see models of this altermodernity in Zapatista struggles and in discussions of "indigenous peoples' conditions" developed in Central and South America, "breaking equally with any fixed dialectic between modern sovereignty and antimodern resistance."[42] What is most interesting for my inquiry is that the altermodern movement shines a light on the essential link between the ideas of modernity and colonization. This is no accident but a case of the two being the same idea. At the same time, nonetheless, altermodernity critiques the return to a largely fantasmagoric tradition based on identity. It performs a set of sidesteps, one of which interests me in par-ticular because it concerns the forms of community, so affected by the theorization of historical time. Thus, according to Hardt and Negri, a "multitude-form" comes to substitute for a "class-form" in the passage from modernity–antimodernity to altermodernity:

> The multitude is a political form of organization that, on the one hand, insists on the multiplicity of social singularities in the struggle and, on the other, seeks to coordinate their com-mon actions and maintain their equality within horizontally structured organizations.[43]

Here again we can discern many of the aspects of the contemporary: meaningful multiplicity, variable groupings, horizontality. More-over, "within altermodernity, a new physiognomy of struggle has made multiplicity a fundamental element in the political project."[44] A final strong connection is the mobile, performative dimen-sion, which, in the vocabulary of Hardt and Negri, is its "constant metamorphosis, its mixture and its movement."[45] Then, why haven't I, right from the very outset of my inquiry, made use of this apparent equation: the contemporary is altermodernity? Perhaps we ought to read on a little further before drawing that conclusion. Hardt and Negri conclude their chapter on altermodernity with a reflection on how the "concepts pose some kind of historical rupture in or with modernity" and "the nature of that break and the possibilities it opens are different in important ways."[46] These concepts are hypermodernity, postmodernity, and altermodernity. I'm in almost complete agreement with the synthesis that they suggest, especially when they say that the rupture between postmodernism and Enlightenment thought resulted only in providing theory with "weak thought and aestheticism,"[47] but I am surprised that they do not initiate a critique of prefixing. None of these concepts related to historical identity are worth holding on to for two reasons: first, using the prefix does not offer a positive kind of content but merely modifies a substantive, in this case, "modernity." Second, none of these concepts can be extricated from Euro- and American-centrism. Each inscribes itself within what both Arjun Appadurai (*Modernity at Large*[48]) and Emily Apter (*Against World Literature*) have called eurochronology. Apter perfectly clarifies the problem when she says that "the categories of 'contemporary' and 'contemporaneity' are particularly susceptible to analysis as period untranslatables that stave off the chronic ageism of periods and epochs."[49] That is, they stave off eurochronology.

This whole series has been about getting free of that. We began by examining the *post-* in order to reveal what lies behind it: a fable reinforcing eurochronology. When we carefully examine the life and death of postmodernity, we see that the fable conceals a much more complex reality. Certainly we recognize that after World War II, it was time to rethink historic nomenclature. But from hypermodernity to altermodernity, passing through postmodernity, we continue, at all costs, to maintain eurochronology in two ways: first, by positioning ourselves in relationship to modernity, and second, by maintaining that sequentiality in temporal representation that is essential to European modernity. The same problem arises with the text that Nicolas Bourriaud wrote for the triennial of the Tate Modern, a text he organized under the rubric of "Altermodern." The text is an interesting one with regard to its major key words, such as *archipelago, heterogeneity, heterochronology,* but the question remains, Why this use of a prefix, if we are actually changing the paradigm?

In this sense, a new terminology would be useful, and we can only rejoice in having passed the age of prefixes. And in making that change, we have implicitly recognized that there is no single, imperial representation of temporality.

Institutions

CRITIQUE OF ART: THE VERTIGO OF INSTITUTIONALIZATION, NEW YORK, 2009

At this stage of our inquiry, the reader might be wondering why there has been no discussion about the critique of art. While the first series, concerning exhibitions, ended with the Western-bourgeois anti-Utopia of everything becoming contemporary art, the third series reviewed the Habermassian myth (not entirely unfounded) according to which the critique of art, which is born as a critique of contemporary art, existed prior to not only the political debate but all modern societies, while more intuitively, one has the impression that there is a metonymic relationship between contemporary art and the semantization of the contemporary—all of which makes it seem odd that the critique of art has not yet formed part of the conceptual debate. But once the topic was broached, the debate hovered for a long and productive time on the basic meaning of the term, expressed in the dominant language, English. In this case, the contemporary is the outcome of a difficult controversy, for its meaning is never given but instead always emerges from a debate. As will be seen, the "emergent" regions are laughing at the old Europe–United States axis, seeing it as a kind of NATO of thought. In one sense, the shape of this debate is the same as those in the preceding series. Central authorities try to contain brouhaha by assigning it to the modern paradigm, but they end up getting overthrown. But the story in this case is clearer, more obvious, and even more brutal than it was in those other domains.

The first authority in this case was the very influential periodical *October,* which, in 2009, published a questionnaire titled "The Contemporary," thereby opening up a controversy over the word *contemporary* in art. This controversy is important because of the tendency to make contemporary art into the emblem of the contemporary. Those who began it had no idea that they would be outpaced twice, first by a rival periodical, *e-flux Journal,* and then a second time by the review affiliated with the Asian Art Archive, *Field Notes.* Let's start with some background. *October* was born in 1976, out of a rift between the editorial staff of the no-less influential review, *Artforum,* which had been the spearhead for modernism. From a triumphant modernism, the new review raised the banners of what was called postmodernism. Interestingly, this change marked another transformation, in this case of the location for speaking about art: from a periodical that was more or less addressed to the general public, to an academic review, from the commercial system to that of the university presses (a similar kind of institutional movement will accompany the contemporary). This new distinction confirms that the postmodern is more a matter of renewed and redoubled distinctions than of their elimination. Another thirty years would have to pass before the theoretical question of the contemporary would be posed, and when it finally was, it was posed in the form of a questionnaire. Hal Foster was the author, recognized by those who tended to read aesthetic theory and art criticism as belonging to the postmodernist movement. And in fact, the form of the questionnaire is hyperallusive, making one think of its use by the surrealists.

The formulation is still partly tentative: the contemporary is presented like a floating category that, paradoxically, has become institutionalized. These modalities are the most interesting:

> This questionnaire was sent to approximately seventy critics and curators, based in the United States and Europe, who are identified with this field. Two notes: the questions, as formulated, were felt to be specific to these regions; and very few curators responded.[1]

These details appeared in a note, and they suggest a problem—which is perhaps why they were put in a note. We regularly see the contemporary moment in art presented as a moment of globalization and of the triumph of the curator, two ways of bringing the mixture to life. But what should we think of a questionnaire that poses the question with a specifically Western focus ("the United States and Europe") and that seems to have de facto excluded curators (though, to be sure, this was not done on purpose)? This is because the issues are different, issues that we have not encountered up until now. The issues involved which institutions, whether academic ones or museums, will have most weight in answering the question, and the identities of the respondents make it quite clear. Out of the thirty-one people who contributed to this issue of the review, only four do not have some university position. The twenty-seven others teach art history or a neighboring discipline in the most prestigious universities and museums in the United States. Only three work outside the United States—one in England and two in Germany. The skewing is thus much stronger than the explanation suggests (and that skewing says something about prestige, the assignment of positions, the control of speech), to the extent that "Europe" provides less than a tenth of the responses and is reduced to the two countries most closely integrated with the United States in matters concerning the art world.

All of the responses to the questionnaire placed the issue of the institution at the center of things. All the initial articles see the category of "contemporary art" as a kind of problem posed to the institution that bears the responsibility for the transmission of knowledge (the university); the problem as posed asks how this category of "contemporary art" will be transmitted and situated within the university academic system, and more specifically the U.S. university (this is not explicitly stated, but for the actors involved, it seems that other international varieties of models for higher education don't matter and that the only model of the university system that is of import, particularly in regard to this question, is the U.S. academic model). We can see in this a very emphatic signal of the tendency of universities in the United States to turn every question into an academic one, an institutional one, a tendency that has both drawbacks and benefits. One drawback is that the ivory tower is vertiginous, as if no other knowledge systems existed outside the academy. One benefit is that institutional critique, which has become an almost dominant intellectual modality, encourages a reflexivity that would otherwise be lacking. Under these conditions, the contemporary appears less as an object and more as a particular way of knowing, which takes itself as its object. It is thus much more than a periodization within the history of art: it constitutes a reconstruction of that history, based upon certain relatively coherent principles. So we see that, whatever plan is used for its placement, the contemporary appears less as a period and more as a critique of a certain form of knowledge, one that makes periodization its cornerstone.

This institutionalization of the question, its nonhistoricity, or rather its nonhistoricizing historicity, in part repeats the limitations implied by the questionnaire, and most notably its Western bias. There were two Nigerian respondents, though they work primarily in Europe and the United States, and who, rather than being art critics, had the defining characteristics of being curators and artists, which led to a break in the cycle of reflexivity (how postmodern!) whose responses are used to remind us of the always ever-present underlying political issues. One of them, the star curator Okwui Enwezor, is becoming a major thinker on contemporaneity, if we consider the number of references other contributors made to his exhibitions and to the 2008 book he coedited with Nancy Condee and Terry Smith.[2] But I would like to focus instead on a work by the second respondent, Chika Okeke-Agulu—at once artist, curator, and art historian, dividing his time between art institutions and a private, prestigious university in the United States. He encourages us to observe the existence of multiple sites of production, transaction, and discourse relative to contemporary art outside the Europe–United States axis. The history of art, he writes, has been transformed by the development of biennales (and other similar large international art exhibitions held in various locales) of contemporary art in regions previously considered peripheral and by the arrival of many artists and theorists from these peripheries. The contemporary is seen as a period of crisis or of tension between a Western discipline and a largely global production. But this very globalization must be understood as having two distinct sides: simultaneously, a globalization and a challenge to the *same,* notably in the aesthetics of the biennale. It reintroduces a kind of periodization, but in a pluralistic and agonistic manner. Following Okeke-Agulu, another important theorist of contemporary art, Terry Smith—author of articles, of a collective book, and of a personal one, all on the subject—distinguishes three large, interconnected currents that characterize the contemporary as a historical moment: globalization, decolonization, and the unprecedented growth of a media- and image-based economy. The periodical is thus marked by this doubleness, quite typical of contemporary theories: on one hand, a reflexive and institutional tendency of comprehending the contemporary (linked to the postmodern Western and largely based in universities in the United States), and on the other, a more historicist and political tendency (typical of countermodernities, or rather, of altermodernities[3]).

We could very well nuance this distinction and enrich it with a detailed reading of the contributions, but it seems to me to be reasonably well accounted for by the questionnaire as a whole, and even more so by the critique of art that is deployed in academic contexts.

This first moment of inquiry into the contemporary in the field of art is important and long overdue. Overdue because, it needs to be said, the semantization of the contemporary over the last few decades took place following a progressive symbolic domination of the visual arts and art exhibitions over other artistic practices, to the rhythm of a certain invasion of art into all aspects of life. Is this addressed in the questionnaire? Not at all. The real stakes seem to be elsewhere. One can imagine it beginning as soon as attention began to be paid to speech. But apart from the larger public, this questionnaire on the contemporary came, as I've said, from an influential university periodical, the fruit of a rupture from a magazine devoted to the general public *(Artforum)*. And it is entirely obsessed with the American university world, which is only a world at all on the condition of ignoring everything that surrounds it. So it's not surprising that, for this very homogeneous population, the questions that the contemporary poses seem to be essentially institutional ones. This point goes well beyond reflections on the contemporary and touches on a particular configuration of current theory.

In his study of "new critical thought," Razmig Keucheyan[4] notes that since the 1970s, intellectuals involved in critical thought are usually disconnected from unions and political organizations. They are most often university professors, and of those, most are university professors in the United States. This marks a break in the history of critical thought and is not without consequences for the theories that they have developed, which have a strongly circular tendency. We could make the same observation about writers, artists, creators, and critics. There is a worldwide tendency toward academic institutionalization of these different productions of knowledge. And yet, not only are these places that adopt them somewhat utopic and cloistered, but these places are their own worlds, or at least microcosms, worthy of our attention. At the heart of these worlds is the institutionalization of knowledge itself and the power games associated with it. On the plus side, this had led to an institutional critique of considerable scope, comparable to the critique the art world underwent in the 1970s. But on the negative side, this critique has been entirely reflexive, its political dimension centered entirely on itself and almost entirely discursive. It reproduces isolated discourses that seem to have nothing to do with the contemporary. Most striking of all is the fact that this first questionnaire, from *October,* is itself a mechanism for controlling speech, a mechanism coming from the institution of universities in the United States. Without intending to, *October*'s questionnaire opened the door to an intense controversy.

THE DOUBLE CONTEMPORARY, SHANGHAI/BERLIN, 2009

The first stage of the controversy in the field of art critique originated with the new review *e-flux Journal.* During its ten years of existence, it devoted successive issues to the question, "What Is Contemporary Art?"[5] Clearly the question is not always the same: *contemporary* reverts to being an adjective attached to a substantive. But there are many reasons to mention these issues. On one hand, the question is in dialogue with *October,* for one of the people who came up with the idea was Anton Vidokle, who had responded to the New York review (and we should note that this is a rare case of a person with no American university affiliation), while Hal Foster contributed to the *e-flux* inquiry with a sampling of the responses he had received, sounding more than a little discouraged:

> As you can see, the questions are directed at critics and cura-
> tors based in North America and Western Europe; I hope they
> do not appear too provincial as a result. I have arranged the
> extracts with an eye to connections that exist between them.

My purpose here is simply to suggest the state of the debate on "the contemporary" in my part of the world today.[6]

The limitations that Foster imposes on himself are remarkable: "my part of the world today." The concurrence of topic in the two publications resembles at best a passing of the torch and at worst a real competition. Here, however, it's no longer a question of remaining limited to respondents from the university and "Euro-Americanism." While the *October* review very clearly valorized a reflexive and institutional approach, *e-flux* lays claim to a historicist approach. The publication followed in the aftermath of a symposium that took place in Shanghai, SH Contemporary, which placed it within the framework of the globalization of the contemporary, or of the contemporary as globalization, described by some of the respondents to the *October* questionnaire. The symposium participants, and those who contributed to the *e-flux* survey, were themselves representatives of that "globalization." We might notice that Hal Foster and Martha Rosler were the only Americans and that only the former has a university affiliation. Other participants came from Mexico, India, Slovenia, Vietnam, China, Switzerland, Germany, and Austria. Almost all of them had passed through—in one manner or another—Berlin, which seems to be dethroning New York. And they speak with that voice that Euro-Americans call, sometimes with contempt, the *biennalization* of the world. Here we can listen to the voices speaking—the voices that *October* spoke about.

If their introduction written for two special issues of the review seems traditional enough, given the presuppositions we have explored earlier, the responses themselves suggest a vision we have not yet tried to sketch. For many, this involves a certain violence, an agonistic stance so far unseen in our inquiry, which implies the difficulty of doing away with the modern hypothesis about the contemporary, and only the third questionnaire fully succeeds in conceptualizing that point: this third one originated with the Asian

Art Archive (whose review is *Field Notes*). The text by the Mexican curator and art critic Cuauhtémoc Medina ("Contemp[t]orary: Eleven Theses") is representative of this tendency. For Medina, the contemporary, in the best case, would be an all-out attack on the modernist Western travesty, what he calls "NATO art":

> Art becomes "contemporary" in the strong sense when it refers to the progressive obsolescence of narratives that concentrated cultural innovation so completely in colonial and imperial metropolises as to finally identify modernism with what we ought to properly describe as "NATO art."[7]

But if there is a strong sense of contemporary, there is also a weak one, which would be the cultural contemporary, linked to the leisure industry:

> In a compelling and scary form, modern capitalist society finally has an art that aligns with the audience, with the social elites that finance it, and with the academic industry that serves as its fellow traveler. In this sense art has become literally *contemporary,* thanks to its exorcism of aesthetic alienation and the growing integration of art into culture. When, by the millions, the masses vote with their feet to attend contemporary art museums, and when a number of cultural industries grow up around the former citadel of negativity, fine art is replaced by something that already occupies an intermediary region between elite entertainment and mass culture. And its signature is precisely the frenzy of "the contemporary": the fact that art fairs, biennales, symposia, magazines, and new blockbuster shows and museums constitute evidence of art's absorption into that which is merely *present*—not better, not worse, not hopeful, but a perverted instance of *the given.*[8]

On this point, Medina's text is very caustic, and it evokes a pandemic of contemporaneity in relationship with global capitalism. The world of art becomes a kind of profane global religion whose principal aim is to make the contemporary manifest. But this same global pandemic contains the seeds of methods of resistance, all of which, Medina says, emerge from the peripheries, or rather out of the end of the representation of geocultures[9] in terms of center and periphery. Yet this political dimension is itself dialectical:

> By the same token, it is no coincidence that the institutions, media, and cultural structures of the contemporary art world have become the last refuge of political and intellectual radicalism. As various intellectual traditions of the left appear to be losing ground in political arenas and social discourses, and despite the way art is entwined with the social structures of capitalism, contemporary art circuits are some of the only remaining spaces in which leftist thought still circulates as public discourse.... It would seem that, just as the art object poses a continuous mystery—a space of resistance and reflection leading towards enlightenment—so do the institutions and power structures of contemporary art also function as the critical self-consciousness of capitalist hypermodernity.[10]

This poses some problems, for this radicalization of art and the constant politicization of its practice can appear like one of the symptoms of what Medina calls the "banality of the present." This passage is certainly the most political and the most dialectical of the two issues; it is representative of that part of contemporary artistic production (including its critics) that presents itself as a kind of antidote (and symptom, as well) for the sick body into which it has been introduced—the sick body of modernity, of culture, of global capitalism. This is also the group that insists the most on the ambivalence of contemporary art, in three contradictory senses: it signals the critique of Eurocentric narratives of modernity; it evokes the integration of art into the culture industry; and finally, in the most ambiguous and most debatable sense, it views the art called contemporary as a form of resistance within the heart of late capitalism—but also as the only, the last, and perhaps doomed form of resistance.

THE "BIENNALIZATION" OF THE WORLD

That second sense deserves some attention, because it lies just be-
low the surface of my essay and of many debates as well. My study
opened with a horizontality that, in the eyes of those who continue
to uphold the old distinctions, is far from being any proof. In fact,
the idea of a weak contemporary, a cultural one like the one Medina
describes in his text, not only connected to the alienation of global
capitalism but also sharing in the "soft power" of that same global
capitalism: this idea has been present in theoretical discussions
since the Second World War (since so-called mass culture escaped the control of the upholders of this distinction), especially
in the form of a controversy over the relation between culture and
spectacle. We encountered this idea already in our first series, in
the form of everything becoming contemporary art. We need to
examine this more closely, for it forms one of the nodes of dissensus
in developed societies (in both economic and inegalitarian terms)
and, eventually, in those societies we call "developing."

With this node, the most obvious signs can be—probably because they're so obvious—the most misleading. For example, it's
easy to see how global capitalism has metabolized the values associated with the worlds of art. We can find a trace of this in the
reconfiguration of the workplace, which has increasingly been
touting, like so many fetishes, values derived from the practice of
art: creativity, autonomy, projects, reviews . . . [11] This reconfiguration
has spread to the new economy, which presents itself, at least in its
most privileged spheres, as a kind of parody, aping the art worlds
in both their modern configuration (individuality, originality,
genius) and their contemporary (relational practice, ateliers, projects, creative collectives)—an imitation that is nevertheless more
powerful, more pragmatic, and more visible than the worlds that
inspire it. A reverse kind of haunting is visible within the art worlds,
which have a strong tendency to present themselves, for example,

within the aforementioned apparatus of "biennalization" (what the art historian Bernard Lafargue called the "Venice syndrome"), as the very spearhead of globalized capitalism: a highly speculative market, selling a single universal model of culture-entertainment.[12] Selling—that is, synchronizing the art world to the same clock and therefore homogenizing it.

Now, as we have already seen, this "biennalization" is one of the phenomena that is emblematic of the contemporary, one which concentrates almost all the controversies surrounding it, especially for those who hold the contemporary in contempt. Not to add my voice to the chorus, but we must remember that a biennale is a method of exhibition, designated by a term related to temporality, implying both periodicity and synchronization. And moreover, a biennale is an event within a specific location. Four variations, then, on the theme of the contemporary (not to mention the three classical unities: place, time, and action).

Anyway, these biennales did not just suddenly spring up over the last twenty or thirty years; rather, they were one of the ways to exhibit recent artwork going all the way back to the nineteenth century, in the form of universal exhibitions or world's fairs, most famously the one of 1855 in Paris, when an international art exhibit was organized in terms of "schools" but was undermined by individualism (as with the "Courbet pavilion"). It was the 1855 World's Fair that (as a means to continue the existence of the salons) became the model for the mother of all biennales, the Venice biennale, which began in 1895. Thus, right next to the public apparatus of the museum and the private apparatus of the market, arose another apparatus, deeply connected since its very beginning to the growing tourism and leisure industries and presuming to synchronize the entire world's time with a single event—as, later, the great sporting events would also do. The biennale is a chronotope, a space-time of concentration, close neighbor to world's fairs and globalized sports events. They form the "Greenwich meridian" of contemporary art, to use the metaphor of Pascale Casanova, who was speaking of literature.[13] And as Pascale Casanova said, this reference point, this meridian, inscribes a temporality of the present. The metaphor of the Greenwich meridian is perfectly adapted to modernity, assuming a singular temporality that imposes itself upon others, a temporality marked by constant self-renewal. But such ideas no longer make sense when biennales begin to multiply, to the point where there's a different one every week in some corner of the globe.

Just as the apparatus of the museum hardly exists any longer in its modern configuration, that of the biennales has also been profoundly transformed: it has become turbulent. And this turbulence poses a real problem for representations of the modern imaginary of art. We infer that we would be living (note the conditional verb) in the era not just of the biennalization of art but also of our very forms of living. To the extent that from now on almost every town is planning a biennale, we can say that this biennalization contributes to making everything art. But what does it mean to say this is a world in which everything is art (that cliché, which I keep at a distance)? And why so much opposition, so much aggression, from those who disdain the idea of everything being art? (The level of aggression is the same whether they come from the right or the left, from a conservative or progressive stance.) After all, haven't we been boasting of the aesthetic qualities in our lives? Why, in the case of biennalization, which would make the world into a space where everything is art, does this seem to lead to some apocalypse whose end we must all fear?

There are at least two possible interpretations, which more or less repeat the same controversy and propose a critique of the contemporary. The first one is always-already Platonic (will we ever escape from it?). There is a real world and a world of appearances. The biennalization of the world turns the real world into a world of appearances and turns reality into a spectacle. And this spectacle is a tool for political domination. In this case, contemporary art is a sort of additive to alienating political forces. Post-Adorno thought, and then post-Debord, represents this same tendency (despite the differences in their *post-*). This line of thought distinguishes two worlds, which are two chronotopes: *the real world, genuinely present* (politics); *the fictional universe of appearances* (culture)—which recalls the opening lines of Debord's *The Society of the Spectacle*:

> The whole life of those societies in which modern conditions of production prevail presents itself as an immense accumulation of spectacles. All that once was directly lived has become mere representation.[14]

The real time of decisions is different from the empty time of mere seeming: Debord says, "The reality of time has been replaced by its publicity."[15] Or, in other words, to return to Agamben citing Barthes, "the contemporary is the untimely." This is a familiar movement. It provides a practical method for studying the empire and the ascendancy of contemporary art. To the extent that the Debord formula continues to use aesthetic vocabulary in analyzing the world of domination, it is not hard to understand that the "Venice syndrome" has become real, at a level never achieved by any Debordian prophecies. And, following *Kulturkritik* instead, we must distinguish art from culture within the aesthetic sphere and realize that art, or rather, Art, is degraded in culture, or rather, in cultures.

Although these antispectacle and anticultural currents of thought offer no explicit theorization of the contemporary, one idea about the contemporary crops up everywhere, denouncing it as the synchronization of fictive subjectivities within the framework of pseudo-events. In this case, the contemporary is distinguished from the present, from presentness, as the representation of presentation. This dialectic is extremely pervasive, at least in Europe. It is what, politically, allows for the union of antidemocratic thought from both the left and the right, democracy being constantly described as the spectacular regime of representation. Hatred of representation and of democracy are consubstantial within this logic, which forms the heart of the contemporary anticontemporary. The contemporary is thus inscribed within a sequence, elaborated at first within *Kulturkritik*, wherein one finds spectacle, democracy, and most certainly culture. Unlike the U.S. approach, this one has the advantage of not disconnecting the theory of art from the political and of avoiding autoreflexivity. Less conveniently, it can never quite get out of the cave; that is, it can never stop making distinctions and separations (is anything more distinct than a cave?), bolting a modern theory of interpretation down upon contemporary phenomena.

Such is the European impasse.

It is easy to get out of this impasse by underlining how the "cultural whole" is nothing more than the greatest indifference to making distinctions between modes of existence, between art and life, between spectacle and action, and so on. And those who condemn it are the heirs of a philosophy of distinction, one that assigns places and assigns roles. Those who wish that the times were not so precisely divided up are the anticontemporaries *(mé-contemporains)*. Readers of Jacques Rancière will recognize his vocabulary here, which he employs as much in political philosophy as in matters of aesthetics. According to him, politics does not come down to the opposition friend–enemy; it's not a matter of a real and authentic world opposed to the world of images and spectacle. Politics is thus a matter of a "distribution of the sensible," or rather, of a "dissensus" over a particular distribution of the sensible, assigning a place to each person. Now, the most impassioned element of Rancière's thought, far more subtle than those who despise the contemporary turning everything into art, is that the distribution of the sensible arises from the aesthetic, which is nothing more than "a delimitation of spaces and times, of the visible and the invisible, of speech and noise, that simultaneously determines the place and the stakes of politics as a form of experience."[16] This is exactly the contemporary imaginary of time that I have been trying to describe in this essay. This is the yardstick with which aesthetic practices can be measured and conceptualized. It is not a matter of lamenting, in a facile Western manner, a world where culture and the kingdom of appearances have replaced the authenticity of politics but rather of studying the system of sensible forms on which politics is founded. Therefore there is no degradation in politics becoming art or culture. And there is no longer any fundamental distinction between spectacle and action, spectacle and life:

> Being a spectator is not some passive condition that we should transform into activity. It is our normal situation. We also learn and teach, act and know, as spectators who all the time link what we see to what we have seen and said, done and dreamed. . . . We do not have to transform spectators into actors, and ignoramuses into scholars. We have to recognize the knowledge at work in the ignoramus and the activity peculiar to the spectator. Every spectator is already an actor in her story; every actor, every man of action, is the spectator of the same story.[17]

Now, it is precisely in artistic practices that we can see most vividly "the blurring of the boundary between those who act and those who look; between individuals and members of a collective body."[18] This describes precisely not only what *contemporary* means in art but also a great many of the new forms of existence.

INDISTINCTIONS: THE RAQS MEDIA COLLECTIVE, SARAI, NEW DELHI

This blurring is not theoretical, nor is it virtual. Nor is it reserved exclusively for the members of the Western club—quite the contrary. If I were to take the time to go and observe all the various actors mentioned in this essay, the Delhi Raqs Media Collective would be the clearest representation of that "blurring of the boundary between those who act and those who look, between individuals and members of a collective body." And no one else has gone further than they have in their investigation of the contemporary, in its artistic and curatorial propositions as well as its theoretical texts. This is the group who will allow us to progress to the third questionnaire, pan-Asian, and who escapes from the contradictions within the *e-flux Journal* (in which it was a participant) and stands in opposition to those of *October*.

In this sense, if my inquiry had been one that fetishized examples, one that sought out the exemplary, I would say that the Raqs Media Collective would stand as the main symbol—because it is collective and declares itself as such. Because the words used in describing the constitution of a formation count. A collective is not a group, not a movement, not a community. Even though there's no hiding the fact that the collective is facilitated by three people (Jeebesh Bagchi, Monica Narula, and Shuddhabrata Sengupta), it's essential to emphasize that no function is attributed to any one person, no singularized competency is assigned, no individualized terms or titles are given. The Raqs Media Collective is the expression of a collective that is not, moreover, reducible to the combination of these three founders, since other participants are integrated into its projects.[19] In their numerous and always impassioned theoretical texts,[20] its members continually return to the point that their practice, and thus their collective, is much less the combination of three members and their biographies and much more the network that results from their communication acts:

> We are sometimes asked who does what in the collective, and the simple answer is that we do not believe in a formal division of labour, or in the individual ownership of ideas. It was to resist the particularly deathly alienation of creative work in the media industry based on a fetish of "individual" labour that we forged a collective practice that guaranteed our creative autonomy.[21]

People ask them, Who does what? Naively, one could also ask, What do you do? And even, Where do you situate yourselves? The response is often "in between," or "amid," or "in relation." For this conception of creative work modifies the coordinates. Its concretization no longer passes through objects that establish an identity but rather begins and continues in a germinative process that often leads to an exhibition. Often, but not always, for the exhibition mode does not account for everything that the Raqs Media Collective produces. They are often presented as an artistic or curatorial collective, with that hesitation between the two terms that often characterizes parts of contemporary artistic production—and for which, again, it could stand as the emblem. But they could just as well be presented as a collective of researchers in the human and social sciences, a collective of critical or militant theoreticians. For that blurring of the boundaries is not only between the individual and the collective or the object of the process but also between disciplinary territories and modes of existence. The collective makes a fundamental refusal of the rupture between theory and practice, between thought, action, creation, and reflection. On the contrary, their propositions wager that conversations between practices and methods are more important than any soliloquy could be.[22] They are emblematic, I would say, in the sense that everything in their practice relates to that nonseparation that characterizes the contemporary, that nondistinction that refuses boundaries.

In fact, a statement of principle is less important than the fact that, while the Raqs Media Collective is internationally recognized (Documenta, Manifesta, etc.) as a curatorial and artistic collective, one could say that for the period 2000–2010, one of their main activities was participating in the hybrid Sarai platform within the Center for the Study of Developing Societies, a major research center in New Delhi. Sarai, founded by two media theorists (Ravi Sundarum and Ravi Vasudevan), and Raqs brought together researchers and practitioners to develop a new, public, creative model of research-practice. The activities are extraordinarily diverse (from publication to exhibition, from conversations to teaching, from research programs to interventions in the social fabric), a diversity that promotes a new language suited to engagement in the contemporary world. Again, emblematic.

At the heart of this program, Raqs has proposed its most accomplished project to date (and, significantly, located in Delhi, not in one of the European or American centers of contemporary art to which they are regularly invited): *Sarai Reader 09*: "Projections." The project's title recalls that of a collection of Sarai's major publications, of which this is the most recent.[23] It's another instance of boundary breaking, this time the boundary between publication and exhibition, the meaning of the former term suiting Raqs much better than the second. Indeed, the modalities of the project are structurally very close to those of a scientific publication. Rather than declaring and imposing a curatorial authority while inviting artists and signing them up for an exhibition, Raqs issued an entirely open appeal, representative of that nondistinction between artistic and curatorial practices, research and forms of sociability befitting the contemporary:

> *Sarai Reader 09* is a nine month exhibition that will unfold as a process generative of visions, concepts, speculations and projections which, in turn, make room for heresy, for new modalities of being, for exchanges, relays and interferences. The exhibition will posit a situation of shifting co-inhabitation in a space by many agents and actors, in diverse, multiple, conjoined and contradictory ways.[24]

Multiple, conjoined, and contradictory: three words key to our inquiry. All the more so as, Raqs says, they hope to produce "a new horizon marked by the intersection of art, sociability, research and commentary."[25]

The general scheme of the exhibition concerns forms of knowledge, while the final experience is rather that of artistic practices and temporary autonomous zones. This is not a case of making everything into contemporary art, as the anticontemporary haters never cease to imagine and condemn, but rather of finding an unexplored relationship between the different forms of knowing, of research, and of creation and of different forms of collective experience. If one wanted to use Jacques Rancière's terminology (and he has written on Raqs), one could say that the artistic productions have lost their habitual functionality and that they have constituted a neutralized space-time in which new forms of circulating speech and of the exhibition of the visible have broken off with the ancient configurations of the possible. So it is a matter of a political moment, or of a critical form of art, insofar as *Sarai Reader 09* "reconfigure[s] the landscapes of what can be seen and what can be thought."[26]

Is it any surprise that, over the past few years, the Raqs Media Collective has contributed to the collective thought concerning the contemporary? They have done so through their exhibitions and their artistic productions. Each one is a reflection on the times, and specifically on the present. Their most recent exhibition, *Extra Time,* at the Chronus Art Center in Shanghai, reminds us that temporality is not only the object but also the material and apparatus *(dispositif)* best suited for their creations. But for an earlier exhibition, *Premonitions,* presented in Calcutta in 2011, the collective specified that this work marked their continuing engagement with time and temporality. Their conception of time is one where the present instant reaches us stratified with other temporalities (pasts, imaginaries, alternatives, forms of future anticipations): exactly the nonmodern conception of temporality that we described in our introduction. In short, in the work of Raqs, we can see a desire to free itself from the modernist conception of linear, progressive time.

Moreover, they have made profound contributions to reflection on the contemporary, never hesitating to involve themselves in the great, global theoretical discussion and critique of earlier assumptions. This was notably the case with the round table they organized at the Indian Art Fair of 2012, under the title "Has the Moment of the Contemporary Come and Gone?"[27] This marked a revival of theory from South Asia, the explicit objective of which was to get free of the Europe–United States impasse, symbolically represented by the questionnaire in *October*. This idea of a second time (and even a third time, following *e-flux*) of theoretical reflection became evident when Jeebesh Bagchi said that the contemporary is available for a collective reevaluation. This is close to the postcolonial concept of "writing back."[28] Jeebesh Bagchi also introduced the question by stigmatizing the terms used in the major debate ("by Hal Foster and all types of critical voices"), seeing that debate as defensive, almost conservative and reactionary, as wanting to save art *from* the contemporary, conceived as an "insurrection of capital." This moment, he continued (the moment of political insurrections, but a moment that looks radically different viewed from the cultural approach), is particularly interesting for rethinking the period of the insurrection of capital. But according to Bagchi, who seemed to brush away the preceding debates with a rather casual sweep of the hand, the first theorization of the contemporary, by Hal Foster and others, was melancholic and in a sense conservative, unable to imagine the world to come (we might add that it was also postmodern). Something else appeared instead; other trajectories emerged, notably in Asia. A new *translatio studii*, a new transfer of knowledge.

The propositions of Ravi Sundaram, of Sarai, are clear in their tendency to largely disqualify the two major references to the contemporary—Hal Foster (mostly for the *October* questionnaire) and Giorgio Agamben—in both cases insisting on the fact that the contemporary has been theorized in a very partial manner and that it must be reconceptualized. Sundaram begins by returning to the theories of Hal Foster, characterizing them as melancholic when they describe the contemporary as a delayed reaction to modernism. But this delayed reaction is completely unsuited to the Asian "us" that Sundaram employs: "*What about us in Asia?*"[29] "Us," spoken with no particular pridefulness, qualifies Asia as an up-and-coming continent, the nouveau riche of global capitalism. But all the same, such melancholy concepts seem scarcely adapted to this new situation. "Instead of that melancholy and economic crisis, there is the delirium of the Asian boom," which signals the end of the "occidental millennium." After a critical reading of Agamben's book, synthesizing the three modes of contemporaneity as seen by Western modernism (untimeliness, archaism, obscurity), Sundaram shows that this position is again marked by the imaginary of the end. And it is urgent that we exit that imaginary:

> So what we need to do probably is to shift away from this. I think the idea of the contemporary needs a different debate from the melodrama of the western decline and the Asian arrival.[30]

The traditional Western terms for cultural production have no purchase in Asia, and the theological vocabulary of Agamben is no kind of resource for conceptualizing what's presented there. And what's presented there is the transformation of the old paradigm of the population, the people, the masses, who can be numbered and controlled by the State into a postmediatized population who can no longer be numbered and controlled. We detect here an old, familiar sequence, from thinking about time to thinking about number, or rather, the innumerable:

> So in this post-media present, the old zone of the people has mutated into archivists, archaeologists, media producers, event instigators, event scene producers, artists, destroyers of the old secrets of power.[31]

For Sundaram, we are passing from one archive into another: from the historic archive of modernity to the archive of contemporaneity in our own lives. Innumerable lives, because this technological culture is in the hands of hundreds of thousands of people, including the very poorest. Consequently, Sundaram argues that we abandon the "old terms" of the post-1968 debate on the contemporary, and especially that we abandon the old dialectic of the end and the after-the-end. Enough with nostalgia for a previous world, and enough with nostalgia for a previous book to connect us with our time. Untimely, perhaps, but not necessarily with regard to history.

"THE AND": THE AUGMENTED QUESTIONNAIRE, HONG KONG, 2012

History is not over yet—not the history of the contemporary any more than any others. The movement to reconceptualize (via postcolonial theory) the contemporary, led by Raqs and Sarai, is far from an isolated one, in an art world that is increasingly trending eastward. Evidence of this is in how one can read the entirety of the debate in the first number of *Field Notes,* the review put out by the Asian Art Archive (AAA). This platform, centered in Hong Kong, was launched "in 2000 in response to the urgent need to document and make accessible the multiple recent histories of art in the region."[32] The region in question stretches from New Delhi to Manila, from Lahore to Singapore, from Shanghai to Taipei, from Phnom Penh to Tokyo, from Ho Chi Minh City to Seoul . . . The objective is clear:

> AAA has evolved into a platform that offers the tools to enrich and complicate the way in which the region's art histories are told, and at the same time, challenge dominant global art historical narratives.

The logic in play is, again, postcolonial. Those who are spoken to—those who *are told*—now seize the power of speech to document and secure their own histories (whose multiplicity is affirmed), richer and more complex than the dominant history they set out to challenge. Documenting histories: this is a very different thing from constructing a historical narrative, in a modernist fashion, because the initiators of AAA do not want, in any way, to produce a narrative that unifies them.

The tension is clearly there, and the urgency is also clear. At the heart of the apparatus is an archive, the principal aims of which are to collect and to display. These two operations are political ones, to the extent that it is they who structure the field of the visible, what deserves to be seen and what does not. In this sense, AAA uses a political logic for its work in a global manner, a logic centering on the archive or, rather, on the archives. This is also why the archives are open, with free access. The items that make up the catalog can take many forms. Some are commissioned pieces by artists, curators, or eminent figures in the art world. Others are collaborative and open. Some are the result of a long process, while others document an event and are thus limited in time. The aim is a counterwriting of contemporaneity, not by means of a unifying narrative but by documentation and bringing resources together.

But the archive, the heart of the project, is neither sanctuary nor sacred; on the contrary, it is under constant interrogation. So much so that AAA, like Sarai, is a hybrid platform of experiences (exhibitions, colloquia, symposia, conferences) that are constantly in the process of reconfiguring the very idea of an archive. Among these experiences was the production of theory within the framework of a publication whose first issue presented itself almost as a manifesto of opposition—in fact, doubly oppositional. In a critical manner, it took up and expanded the principle of the questionnaire about the contemporary from the *October* review, in order to show everything that was lacking and what its hidden agendas were. The title was a play on words, more subtle than it first appears: "The And." It suggests a return as well as a surpassing, in opposition to "again" and the "end," showing not only the provincialism of the *October* questionnaire but its imperialism as well, insofar as it only sought the opinions of European and American thinkers, while the nonoccidental world in fact played a very important part in its conceptualization. The really striking thing about the introduction to the questionnaire is that it pleads both for a strong investment in the contemporary and for the deployment of its diversity: semantic diversity, which needs to take into account all the different translations that have been made of the contemporary; contextual diversity, and thus variability; narrative diversity, rendering the multiplicity of histories at play in the region; temporal diversity, since the contemporary is in continual metamorphosis. The only method that will work is the archivist one, as the goals of the organization and of exhibition suggest—and again we must stress, with free access on the Internet. Responses to the questionnaire are organized in the chronological order of their arrival, each of the responses being prefaced with the date and the hour of its arrival. In this way, the questionnaire is very close to the governing ideas in our inquiry. Two main ideas stand out. First, the contemporaneity deployed in south Asia is created with no relationship to some modernity to which it is an afterthought or to which it stands in opposition. Second, the contemporary is a historical concept that frees itself from the teleological historicism of modernity. The result, as one quickly sees, is that Asia presents itself as an observation post for scrutinizing the contemporary that is more relevant than those of the United States or Europe.

ARTISTIC ACTIVISM

What "contemporary" means in the phrase "contemporary art" has produced an exceptionally rich series, accented by the three questionnaires. One can encounter there a publication often presented as post-Marxist but in fact caught in the toils of American scientific ultraliberalism: we have seen how it recentered the critique of the contemporary within the university academic world, with its institutional critique; we have seen how globalization was an effect of its discourse and how it tried to control the turbulences that began to overwhelm it. This is why another publication, a younger one, a less New York–ish and more Berlin-centered one, took up the terms of the debate and opened them to other actors, theorists, and curators working in various institutional and geographic worlds, but taking part in the dialectic of a doubled contemporary, with resignation and resistance to the entirety of culture. That entirety of culture forms, in the old European world, one of the major controversies of the epoch—a controversy that, curiously, resolves itself into a dispute between pro- and anti-Platonists (circling around truth, spectacle, appearance, the political). But there is no resolution for this debate outside of the East, where the collectives of Raqs Media and Sarai in Delhi have become in many respects emblematic of what the contemporary means in art and what it means with regard to forms of existence. They offer a reflection that frees itself from the melancholic historical visions expressed by the two most often cited thinkers in Europe and the United States when the subject of the contemporary arises: Giorgio Agamben and Hal Foster. The gaze of Raqs Media Collective and of Sarai has been turned fully toward Asia, the "region" that has taken over, in the final questionnaire, theoretical reflection on the contemporary, without abandoning it any longer to the impasse of negativity.

This brief summary is instructive about the controversy over the contemporary in art that largely goes beyond the narrow, Gallo-centric quarrel over contemporary art (which is only a small part of the issue). Everything is up for debate: the nature of the contemporary (what is it?), the use being made of it (by whom?), and its location (where is it deployed?). As we know, the first form of the controversy concerned geopolitical issues connected to globalization and could be briefly formulated as, Where is the present of art? Unlike a modernist mysticism that wants the present to have a specific site (we might recall the Nobel Prize–winning Mexican poet Octavio Paz, who, in his *In Search of the Present*,[33] said that as a young man, he had often had the sensation of having been relegated to the margins of the present), the contemporary present is multilocal: it is at the same time in the imperial form of the U.S. institutions, in the European ghosts, and in the counterwriting of the "emerging" regions. The present of the contemporary is controversy—with no solution possible. If I have given more importance to the counterwritings, it is because of their unexpected aspects and the manner in which they are aware of the controversy. But they are not *the* contemporary.

The controversy is more far-reaching than this; we have already encountered it in the first series of our inquiry and by the various formulations that have been repeated since then: there is a metonymic link between contemporary art and the semantization of the word *contemporary*. More specifically, I think that the controversy over the contemporary in art is also a controversy over politics and ways of living, not simply because the world of art can be seen metaphorically as the last stage of late capitalism but because it constitutes the extension, the object, and the conceptual heart of late capitalism. It is the object when political forms make art a tool of propaganda. Contemporary art becomes tourism, like leisure, like the competition between cities vying to become event-cities. It is also the object and the extension when fashion and merchandising make it into a sales pitch, a mark of distinction in the service of the neoliberal bourgeoisie. It is the heart of the matter for those who see the model for a liberal society in these artistic forms of life (styles of work, of social organization). For all these reasons, the controversy over art is above all a political controversy, one of the most powerful and most impassioned that there is. Those who deplore contemporary art, thinking it's a sign of weakening politics in an apolitical epoch, are wrong. Political issues aren't discredited because it is in the art world that they're so strongly expressed. On the contrary, an entire arm of critical theory has made contemporary art its field of investigation for exactly that reason. It arises, perhaps, from the idea that late capitalism uses artistic discourse to produce consensual subjectivities and public spaces for the majority. Producing dissensual public spaces, in the form of temporary autonomies as well as performative subjectivities, contemporary art can present itself as a critique of global capitalism on its own ground. This is why theory, artistic practice, and militant activism are not really separate things.

Archaeology

HISTORICAL LITERACY: SANTIAGO, CHILE, 2011

After that long series concerning the criticism of art, the reader might think that everything has now been said. Of course, a search will turn up multiple semantizations of *contemporary*. But one of these remains implicit and a little hidden, even though it ought to be the most apparent. And with this one (historical temporality), the present study will come to an end—though not to a conclusion. We will get there by returning to the place where we started: South America.

We'll begin with a collection of essays that appeared in Santiago, Chile, titled, naturally enough, *¿Qué es lo contemporáneo?* Its subtitle gets more specific: *Actualidad, tiempo histórico, utopias del presente.*[1] The subtitle problematizes the contemporary by joining it with three of its near neighbors—the current, history, and the present—knowing that these terms may send us back to three disciplinary ensembles: cultural studies, history, and philosophy. Moreover, the book suggests these tensions and these disciplinary intersections very directly by returning in its first lines to the text by Giorgio Agamben (who is quoted, incidentally, in French, which is interesting), but reading it through the lens of cultural studies, which is possible because Agamben is also interested (though we tend to forget this) in pop culture and fashion. In that sense, this reading of Agamben's text is the exact opposite of the kind of reading it would get in France. Instead of valorizing the untimeliness of the dominant culture, the book lays out the contemporaneity of cultural practices running from the theater arts to new forms of communication. The one deals with the modern imaginary, the other with the contemporary imaginary.

The interdisciplinarity of the approach is clear in the two tutelary references, in the introduction, that precede the reference to Giorgio Agamben:

> The project of a publication bringing together works on the contemporary has been implemented under the auspices of the ideal of the open university: a non-bounded space where ideas and interests can interact, whose only law is the equality of intelligences.[2]

Bringing together the contemporary and the open university in the same sentence cannot help but make us think of the British foundations of cultural studies, though the allusion to the equality of intelligences is a direct reference to Jacques Rancière, the philosopher of the contemporary. And so this approach to the contemporary takes account (as does my own), in a more structural way, of the new mass access to knowledge. Opening up, finding intersections, doing away with boundaries, equality—these are the key words that the present study has been using to characterize the contemporary, key words that follow logically from the conclusion of the preceding series.

The first articles interrogate the philosophy of time and respond more freely to the question of what it is to be contemporary, with a more specific variant: "What is it to be contemporary today, in relation to the modern epoch?" A number of concepts come into play: that of the event, borrowed from Deleuze; those of heterochronicity and anachronicity, developed by Didi-Huberman; those of narrative and experience, coming from Paul Ricœur. All these concepts, as we will see, arise from a heterodox approach to historical time. It is not surprising to find here also the ideas of Reinhart Koselleck and of François Hartog, who, in Valderrama's phrase, have made the present into "the temporal matrix that organizes the ensemble of possible histories."[3] The author follows the tendency that is so strong today, at least in Europe and, apparently, in Chile, of approaching history via regimes of historicity. Although Valderrama attempts to separate himself from that body of work, especially by returning to the Nietzschean absolute of the untimeliness of the present, the conceptual framework of the book he edited shows very clearly a coherent vision of historical temporalization beginning with the present—a vision that sees the contemporary epoch as distinguished by an overvaluation of the present, to the detriment of the past and the future. And there is an implication: to take account of the contemporary is above all to do away with linear and sequentialist models of history.

The contemporary comes to present a kind of problem to the structures of knowledge and therefore to institutional structures. As a first step, we can start by thinking about the discipline of history, as Luis G. de Mussy explains:

> Even if people have spoken of a new stage in history since the 1980s, there has been little discussion of how this new denominator of an epoch has transformed or at least redefined the matrix of the discipline and history as an institution. Data and references to the recent past are abundant, but what is lacking is a "historical alphabetization" capable of providing a meaning and an awareness of this other time.[4]

Luis G. de Mussy does not go into this structural level but quite rightly questions the teaching of the contemporary, or rather what the contemporary does to teaching. And in fact, one of the characteristics of the contemporary world from the point of view of its representations is that it has inscribed present objects, contemporary artifacts (e.g., books or works of art), in places that were not previously devoted to them, and specifically institutional places, that is, places that institutionalize knowledge, and notably places devoted to heritage: school, university, museum. Inevitably, the question of the canon gets posed—the question that could be considered the very shape of the epoch, since it involves the criticism and theory of art, as well as literary theory, as well as the discipline of history. Hence the "canon wars" that, in the United States, have opened up new pathways to knowledge beginning in the early 1980s. Flooded by immigrant student populations both Asian and Latin American, U.S. universities became involved in a major controversy regarding what should be taught. Should only canonical European history continue to be taught? And doesn't this process of canonization arise out of a homogenizing fetishization that tries to silence heterogeneous realities? The movement is always the same: the crowds overflow and become overwhelming, ending the illusion of homogeneity.

Historical literacy would open up an active education thanks to "guerilla tactics" regarding the canon. Luis G. de Mussy borrows this idea of guerilla tactics from Idelber Avelar, a Brazilian literary theorist specializing in Latin America in relation to contemporary Chilean historiography and its struggles with the issue of remembrance. This constitutes a double kind of territorializing within the Latin American framework—or rather, it models the problem posed by the contemporary for the discipline of history within a Latin American framework. Thus, while one could await a more classic type of reflection on the necessity of redefining the contemporary as a period within the discipline of history, the author instead invites us to think of the contemporary as a critical gesture, pedagogical and even political, within and through the discipline of history. Following on the international valorization of the regimes of history, this constitutes the Chilean volume's second contribution, and it shapes the two axes of this final series: opposing the contemporary to historicism and calling the processes of canonization back into question.

HISTORIOGRAPHIES OF THE CONTEMPORARY

But in fact the volume goes beyond the state of the discipline of history. It pushes ahead to places the discipline had never gone, and apparently had mostly refused to go. It thus encourages us to go back to the moment when everything could (some would say, should) begin: history, as a discipline. Because if there's any discipline, that is, any form of knowledge and relationship with the world, that poses the question of the contemporary, it's definitely history. But if it poses the question explicitly, using the actual word, at least in English or one of the Romance languages, it's always preceded or followed by a form of theoretical malaise, which is interesting in itself.

Therefore the reader might ask, Why didn't we begin here? More than likely, it was to avoid the lure of a premature answer. Because, as I've said, if we want to engage the contemporary as history, a classic and definitive answer emerges: the contemporary is a period, with boundaries, with beginning and ending dates. The beginning date varies according to national traditions. Often, in Europe, it's 1789. The fact that it varies according to national traditions renders it suspect—smelling of egocentrism and nationalism. And the fact that it would need a concluding date, whether a floating or a fixed one, which would open us up to the possibility of a postcontemporary—this too encourages us to reject definitively the hypothesis of the contemporary as a historical period. Twentieth-century historians have been working continually to delegitimize a historical narrative based on great events, favoring instead one based on continuities, permanencies, *longues durées,* rather than a series of ruptures and of very precise global sequences (the Annales school of historiography is a good example of this tendency). They have also delegitimized the narrative of great actions and great men in favor of a multitude of microhistories, juxtaposed and differentiated (see the phenomenon known as *microstoria*). And there is a second major critique addressed to narrative history, or at least to the caricatural variety, based on its Eurocentrism, not to say its Gallocentrism. Finally, there is a less frequently formulated critique: old-style grand narrative history is epistemologically isolated, since almost no other discipline with a historical dimension (except art history, a discipline that is less and less indentured to history proper), not even literary study, continues to use it. So, that historical narrative that long ago erected a period called "contemporary" has had very little influence on the meaning of the word *contemporary*. For all these reasons, I tend to think that the current debates on the contemporary in history owe more to global contemporaneism than to history and, at the same time, that the construction of history by history—what I am about to term *historicism*—has largely prevented us from conceptualizing the contemporary. And this has provoked in recent years some extremely important historiographical debates. Recently, a historian "of the present time," Henry Rousso, has turned to this intellectual construction and, in doing so, has produced what seems to me to be the first history of the contemporary. According to him, the idea (borrowed from Benedetto Croce) that all history is contemporary history is far from an isolated one. On the contrary, it is the basis of premodern models of history, models that the contemporary conception of history has reanimated. Strangely, or perhaps logically,

> it was at the very moment when contemporaneity began to take root in the mental universe of the nineteenth century that the discipline of history, in the process of being professionalized, decided to separate contemporary history off from the rest of history, granting it a singularity because the identity of the discipline itself was reinforced by that act of exclusion.[5]

A fine chapter follows this, titled "Contemporaneity in the Past," which demonstrates how the old historical models tended not to separate present and past, whereas it was modernity that made that very separation into the disciplinary structure of history. The introduction of this essay showed that making such a separation was the very definition of modernity. And it arises again here. It also constitutes the hermeneutic mode and the ethical posture of history:

> an approach marked through and through by the tension, some-times the opposition between history and memory, knowledge and experience, distance and proximity, objectivity and sub-jectivity, researcher and witness. All these cleavages can exist within the same person.[6]

It will shortly be clear that the abandonment of this posture is in part what leads to the birth of cultural studies, just as it gives birth to the contemporary imaginary of time. And it was from the igno-rance of this posture that ancient history was born, with modern history now seeming like a kind of parenthesis of "detachment," of separation and "objectivity." The historians of the ancient world were contemporaneists in this sense, presenting themselves as ac-tors within the events described, because "the act of narration itself has a political utility."[7] In the same way, in the medieval epoch, it is difficult to distinguish a "historiography of the contemporary" because "the past and the present, the non-contemporary and the contemporary, always co-existed."[8] Several foundational concepts arose during the Renaissance: the separation of past and present and the sequentiality of the past, according to the "sacred division into four historical periods"[9] that modernity instituted: antiquity, the Middle Ages, modern times, and the contemporary epoch. Finally, with the Renaissance arose the definition of the practice of history as distinct from the objects it studies. These foundational concepts in turn produced historicism, a science of the past based upon separation. They produce a strange contemporary, a non-contemporary one, and one that is still with us; it's probably the influence of the discipline of history on the representation of collective time that makes it hard to conceptualize the contemporary. And it is first and foremost against this historicism that the theories of the contemporary will be elaborated, taking the word itself out of the adjectival position, as in "contemporary epoch." The contemporary thus becomes a mode of historical approach that is not historicist.

Many stages are involved in this new constitution of the contemporary. For example, from the center of the discipline, of a world vision, another approach originating in historiography has in fact contributed to the great debate on the contemporary. This approach, already alluded to, is one to which Rousso has frequent recourse, working with the semantics of historical time and coming from the field worked by the historian Reinhart Koselleck. There is in fact a real homogeneity in the way numerous studies characterize the historical and existential regime proper to the contemporary. They all evoke a hypertrophied present, a crisis involving the future or progress, an invasion of the present into the past which can only be seen through the lens of the present, an end to linear time but by no means a return to cyclical time, and so on. François Hartog has written the most insightful books on this, trying to describe the regime of historicity of our epoch. To do so, he forges the concept of presentism, as opposed to better-known approaches centered on either past or future. The premodern periods are globally past-oriented in the sense that they valorize, to an excessive extent, the past or the ideal of reproducing the past. This is the theme of the golden age or of paradise lost. Aesthetically, this reveals itself in the search for perfection through imitation. But the modern regime would be globally futurist, allying socially and politically with the desire for progress and, in aesthetic terms, with the search for the new. Finally, the contemporary regime would see a form of perpetual present evolving. "Everything happens as if there were only the present," says Hartog.

> The present has thus *extended* both into the future and into the past. Into the future, through the notions of precaution and responsibility, through the acknowledgement of the irreparable and the irreversible, and through the notions of heritage and debt, the latter being the concept which cements and gives coherence to the whole. And into the past, borne by similar concepts such as responsibility and the duty to remember, the drive to make everything into heritage, the lifting of time limitations, and last but not least the notion of "debt."[10]

The power of Hartog's book, in the wake of Koselleck's work, lies in proposing a veritable history of the present as a form of experiencing time. The regime of historicity also designates "the modalities of self-consciousness"[11] in relation to human communities. To the extent that my own inquiry on the contemporary has been a reflection on precisely these same modalities of self-consciousness within the human community, Hartog's study is an especially important one for me. Because ultimately, it doesn't much matter knowing which period should be cited for the moment we began to get something of a grip on this self-consciousness.

A bit later, thinkers began to focus on the modalities of aesthetic being-in-time. The word that kept coming up was *spectrality,* a word that suggests the presentism of history. It's found in political philosophy (such as Derrida's *Specters of Marx*) and in literary analysis (such as Jean-François Hamel's *Revenances de l'histoire*). And it comes up in art criticism, for example, in (again) Hal Foster's *The Return of the Real* and *Design and Crime*. In a widely cited text called "This Funeral Is for the Wrong Corpse,"[12] Foster presents a vision very much like that of François Hartog, preceding him by two years in the use of the term *presentism,* though it's not clear that Hartog borrowed it from Foster.[13] So Hartog's book is involved in an ensemble of publications, all very influenced by aesthetic theory, to which his work has given a historical depth. And in fact, history, considered as a discipline, has only been able to give an account of the present by crossing over its own boundaries in search of models that would render temporal awareness intelligible. But these other models continue to use approaches that my study is attempting to undo: the overvaluation of the "after" in theories of the contemporary and the use of the modal approach from an epochal perspective. As we saw clearly enough in our series devoted to the "battle of the *posts*," in our globalized perspective, these approaches can never have more than a temporary usefulness.

ANACHRONISMS

It is necessary to step off the main path, then, in the direction of those "marginal" disciplines, to find a revival of the historical approach to the contemporary. The first attempts were really theories of the historical present rather than models that thought through all the consequences of the critique of sequentiality, periodization, and the epochal approach. It's not a trivial point that they were born from within disciplines that history had often scorned, or at least considered, as subordinate disciplines: art history and archaeology. Not trivial, but perhaps risky, for it was not so much art history and archaeology that produced a theory of the contemporary as it was the influence of Walter Benjamin upon some of those fields' representatives—minorities within their fields, to be sure. In fact, two of the most fascinating theories of time and of the contemporary (though they are not presented in exactly those terms) written in French were by Benjaminian thinkers: the art historian Georges Didi-Huberman and the archaeologist Laurent Olivier.

At first, though, Didi-Huberman's approach would seem to be a critique of the contemporary. It is a critique of the contemporary both as conceived by historicism and as conceived as a period and, most importantly, as euchronism. "The concordance of times," Didi-Huberman writes, "does not exist—almost."[14] Now, as we know,[15] "the concordance of times" is more or less an exact translation of *contemporary*. One might object that "concordance of times" could be understood as a concordance of temporalities, which would invert the meaning, but instead, the concordance Didi-Huberman refers to arises from "euchronic consonance." But just before this phrase, we find the following, which crystallizes a good part of my own inquiry:

> Anachronism traverses all contemporaneities.

Anachronism is another name for *contemporaneity,* in the sense of a co-temporality. What Didi-Huberman's book shows us is that historicism has constructed two fictions of temporality: sequentiality and euchronism. But all reality, and every object, is traversed by multiple times, even if only in the perception of another, who desynchronizes in order to resynchronize them. To use Didi-Huberman's terms, every reality, every object, is polychronic, heterochronic, anachronic. Thinking in the contemporary—let us call it contemporism (a term that includes not just thinking the contemporary but practicing it)—becomes, at this point, a major epistemological issue, leading to a redesign of the theoretical representations of the world: against euchronic contemporism, the art historian argues for an anachronic, polychronic, heterochronic contemporism:

> We find ourselves at the wall, as if facing an object of complex time, impure time: an extraordinary *montage of heterogeneities forming anachronisms.*[16]

But how to implement a science of anachronism? Because "in fact there is no history except that *which follows after the current present.*"[17] And we must think of this currentness as charged with all possible temporalities. Our perspective undergoes a double reversal: both from the past, which we must reascend, to use the curious expression of Rousso, and toward the polychronic present—from sequentiality to polytemporality. In this sense, contemporism offers itself as another way of doing history against historicism. But this is no longer a weak contemporism from a euchronic context, from ephemerality. Its importance is not connected to "presentism" within the frame of historicism; it is important because it no longer uses the fiction of a continuous, homogeneous, sequential time. Above all, though Didi-Huberman does not mention it, this contemporism is in no way opposed to the non-Western counter-writing that we encountered in the preceding chapter. On the contrary, anachronic contemporism is itself a counterwriting.

In any case, it is entirely in phase with the proliferation of mediatized temporalities. The level of simultaneities today is such that this double inversion has never known so great an audience for the ensemble of its representations and theories. And if, back in 2000, Didi-Huberman's book felt like a kind of hermeneutic heterodoxy, fifteen years later, we find that it has affected a great number of historical studies. I'm a part of this movement (while insisting more than some others on the importance of the contemporary), and I'm also inspired by his reading of the work of Walter Benjamin. If one were to characterize this movement, one could say that it's a matter of "taking up again, redesigning from top to bottom, a major issue, that of historicism as such."[18] Or, to put it more precisely, it is historical thinking outside of the discipline of history, or at least outside of its so-called historicist side:

> The issue, for Benjamin, was precisely *to unearth* the models of temporality that were both less idealistic and less trivial than the models then in use, in the historicism inherited from the nineteenth century.[19]

Didi-Huberman says that Benjamin "worked violently against the grain." That grain was that of the historians who "traveled to past times." Time travel is impossible, as science fiction never ceases to tell us. There is no science of the past, and historical inquiry is made in the present, which makes all temporalities contemporary. Including the past, if we want to keep using that term, and including the future—as symptom, as surviving trace, or as prophecy.

This surviving trace, this survival, has nothing to do with the spectrality discussed earlier. That spectrality never called into question the historicist model of successiveness (past, present, future), and it remains associated with the *post-* paradigm, with the *after.* Instead, this survival clearly interrogates linear history. The present is always a resurgence of the past of the *longue durée,* both as symptom and as ancient prophecy in the process of verification. Benjamin and Didi-Huberman essentially evoke the history of art, which should be a history of advents or arrivals and hindsights, though of course both writers know that they're shaping a different way of thinking about historical temporality. In my view, this way of thinking of temporality is precisely what contemporism calls for—keeping in mind that this is in no way a presentism. It does away with linearity, discovering within each object its own "anterior history" as well as its own "ulterior history." It likewise does away with continuity:

> Thus the "reified continuity of history" finds itself entirely exploded: and thus the "homogeneity of the epoch explodes" as well.[20]

Could a more definitive renunciation of the epochal vision of the contemporary be imagined? Blowing up the "false" homogeneity of the epoch thus becomes the mission of the contemporary, and the contemporary becomes the sole observation post from which we can study history. This approach, which I practice as well, has profound consequences, both ethical and methodological. Because it necessarily makes the contemporist into an archaeologist. "*Time is the very matter of things,*"[21] and all things matter, because within them the unconscious of the time lies, and only a material archaeologist will be able to reveal it. This contemporism that we are defending, following Didi-Huberman in his reading of Benjamin, deploys itself in a material archaeology that opens up a psychic archaeology. The model that underlies contemporism, therefore, is not so much a historical as an archaeological one:

> What [Benjamin's] material archaeology brings to light is nothing less than a mythic and genealogical structure: a structure of survivals and anachronisms (in which all genealogical times cohabit within the same present).[22]

The proposition, therefore, is simple. Far from being a science of the past, archaeology is a study of the present—or rather, more precisely: archaeology, within the materiality of the present, lets us discover the memory of the past. The present is the seat of a multidirectional time that goes beyond sequential, linear, historicist time:

> In this perspective, archaeology needs to be redefined as a discipline specifically attuned to the symptoms of material memory.[23]

In a very fine rereading of Michel de Certeau, Laurent Olivier reminds us that traditional historiography makes a sharp division between the past as object of study and the present as site of the inquiry. Now, this division is artificial to the extent that the past only exists when it is reactualized by the present. Olivier says that we must deploy another strategy, another approach to historical time, one that is not based on divisions. Contemporism can become this other strategy, this other approach to the time of history: from historicism to contemporism, from history to archaeology.

This archaeological, contemporist model is now becoming competitive with the linear and sequentialist model. For the moment, we mainly see it in artistic practice. Thus the exhibition halls have, for a number of years lately, welcomed the ideas that invite a heterodox rereading of history, in favor of a contemporist archaeology. Archaeology itself, the dig, the person with pick and shovel—these have become recurrent figures in contemporary art (and in the postures adopted by writers). But what about critical discourse? How can I use this as, for example, a literary theorist? I can learn to distrust sacred objects. I can interest myself in trash, in what is discarded, in remains, in the surface of things. I can take a materialist approach to literary history and its subjects. Renounce historical continuity, favor the effects of discontinuity, make untimely connections, practice learning through montage. Stay as close as possible to the emergence of the present insofar as it can point toward the fundamental form of the relation possible between the Now (the instant, the flash) and the Other Times (which exist in latency, or in fossil form), a relation the traces of which will be kept by the Future (in tension, in desire).[24] It is a program (difficult, because so utterly opposed to our usual practices) that must be achieved, following those who have gone before. And it's not at all a bad thing, at this point in our inquiry, to see a program begin to take shape.

HETERODOX HISTORIES

Let's reaffirm this point: exhibition spaces have, over the past few years, welcomed ideas that invite a heterodox rereading of history, in favor of a contemporist archaeology. There is plenty of evidence to satisfy anyone interested in the exhibition world. For me, it's enough to turn back to my immediate environment to see it. For several years now, with a great deal of publicity, the most prestigious galleries have been carrying on a critical reevaluation of the orthodox history of modern art, invented by Alfred H. Barr of MoMA on the historicist model. At exactly the same time, the Centre Pompidou and the Tate Modern were doing similar work. The Pompidou had the privilege of engaging in a feminine rewriting of art history in a new exhibit from its permanent collections comprised entirely of work by women (with the title *elles@centrepompidou*). At the Tate Modern, Nicolas Bourriaud, charged with designing the triennial, suggested the title *Altermodern*, to evoke an exit from modernity. These two exhibitions were powerful gestures (especially the former), and very visible ones, too—though it's true that both fit in well with the more general trend. But they brought orthodoxy into question without managing to reverse its hermeneutic principles. So *elles@centrepompidou* upheld the ideology of the modernist exhibition and the modernist vision of history, while inverting its political dimension (which is, of course, not trivial). As for *Altermodern,* it revealed a sequentialist and epochal view of history, the kind we are familiar with from our preceding chapter.

Alternatively, a wide curatorial and artistic movement was rethinking exhibition as a historical inquiry, contesting the historicist model and moving toward the archaeological and contemporist one. So, again, turning to my own immediate environment, two recent exhibitions have suggested fascinating ideas concerning history. The first, *Les fleurs américaines* (American flowers), was held at the Plateau art center, under the direction of Yoann Gourmel and Élodie Royer, running from December 13, 2012, to February 17, 2013:

> "Les fleurs américaines" [the leaflet tells us] set in motion some facts and strategies that contributed to defining art in the twentieth century. In this sense, it was not an exhibition of modern art, but *a contemporary exhibition concerning the construction of the history of modern art,* and the manner in which the latter has continued to define the criteria of art today.[25]

Much more than the mainstream exhibitions mentioned earlier, this one, proposing an archaeological strategy, made the visitor feel the force of the cultural propaganda that the apparatus of orthodox exhibition had deployed, an orthodoxy that took shape in the years before the Second World War and with MoMA. Thus the visitor discovered the Salon de Fleurus, an exact replica of Gertrude Stein's salon—Stein, the collector of "souvenirs of modern art." Next, the visitor to this fictional dig encountered a scale model of MoMA itself, such as Alfred H. Barr had conceived it. The narrative thread of the exhibition—well adhered to throughout—was a journal kept by a connoisseur-traveler-archaeologist embarking on a study of modern art. So several historical models came into play, under the patronage of a Walter Benjamin who here became a fictional character. It was not a matter of laying out other histories but rather of other forms of making history intelligible. This wasn't the first show put on by this curatorial duo, for several years before, they had produced an exhibition based on Agamben's *Qu'est-ce que le contemporain?* (titled *The Crystal Hypothesis*) and a series of lectures titled "On This and That: Notes on Conceptual Art from the Year 1000 to Our Day." They have formed a sort of brotherhood of heterodoxy among curators and historians of art with the American Museum of Art in Berlin, the Salon de Fleurus in New York, and the Triple Candie collective.

At the same time—still remaining within my own immediate environment—another curatorial duo used the Deleuzean title "A People Is Missing" for a more political version of the archaeology of the contemporary. In a series of exhibitions, they interrogated the way history is made, not only from a counterhistoric, postcolonial, and queer point of view, but also from a heterodox one—that is, by interrogating the hermeneutic modes themselves. For example, their "Atlas Critique" not only produced an atlas of critical thought but more importantly questioned the atlas as a counterhistorical form of knowing (guided by Didi-Huberman, who was in turn guided by Aby Warburg[26]). Thinking about the spatial aspect of contemporaneity, with space dominating time, the curators presented works that reconfigured historical and political topics via cartography, the atlas, montage, and other spatial representations. I only discovered their work toward the end of my study, but the reader will understand at once that the contemporism that I advocate can be seen in this spatial turn in theory, as a contesting of the historicist paradigm. Kantuta Quirós and Aliocha Imhoff remind us of Foucault's marvelous concept of heterotopia:

> The present epoch will perhaps be above all the epoch of space. We are in the epoch of simultaneity: we are in the epoch of juxtaposition, the epoch of the near and far, of the side by side, of the dispersed. We are at a moment, I believe, when our experience of the world is less that of a long life developing through time than that of a network that connects points and intersects with its own skein.[27]

Foucault returns us to the principles of my study and guides us toward its end. I have followed his recommendation to write a general history as opposed to a global one. A general history deploys itself within a space of dispersion. But within this well-known text, Foucault tells us often that ours is the time of simultaneities, and that simultaneity implies juxtaposition, and that therefore a montage is preferable to a monologic discursivity. Only now can I see that my own organizational protocol obviously reproduces those of the historical inquiry that took place in exhibition spaces, protocols that have in common a delinearization of the writing of history. And so another genealogy of historical models is brought to light. Besides the Benjaminian constellation alluded to earlier, I must mention a set of heterodox thinkers whose work deserves reevaluation. This is the case with Manuel DeLanda, an American philosopher originally from Mexico associated with the project called "A People Is Missing," as well.[28] I think also of Svetlana Boym, who influenced a great many artists, notably the Raqs Media Collective and the Albanian video artist Anri Sala.

And one would have to be blind not to notice a plural, dialectical coherence, sometimes oppositional, a historical strategy, that goes from presentism (Hartog) or spectrality (Foster and Derrida) to anachronism and polychronism (Didi-Huberman and Olivier) and on to nonlinearity (DeLanda, Boym, and the artists of the Raqs Media Collective). This coherence makes the contemporary into an observation site and a field of action that unsettles modern historicity, with its linear and sequentialist narrative. And one would also have to be blind not to see that these latter ideas, those that have most attracted my attention, have come from marginal disciplines, open to other methods and practices and other sites for expression. This ensemble is what I would like to call *contemporism*.

BIRTH: BIRMINGHAM, 1964

This contemporism should not overshadow another one to which it can readily be connected, and of which it is, in some respects, the heir (as am I, I freely admit). This other contemporism runs throughout this book, and it is therefore appropriate to conclude with it: I refer to cultural studies. I haven't forgotten that the first research center to include both the word and the concept of the contemporary in its name was the Centre for Contemporary Cultural Studies, in England, at the University of Birmingham in 1964. I don't want to go into the history, but I will simply say that the contemporary had to make its way into institutions by breaking and entering, slipping into the margins, via evening courses taught by politicized theorists and professors. These are the ones who brought together artistic practices with social and individual ones into an ensemble they called "culture." They shook up the field of knowledge, decentered it profoundly, and then, though they were themselves deeply Anglocentric, authorized a new approach to contemporaneity, one much more in phase with the forces that were shaping it.

So much has been made of the word "cultural" in the title

that almost no one has remarked or written much about the use of the word "contemporary." Now, the great epistemological split that developed in Great Britain during the 1960s is just as much a product of the development of contemporary studies as it was of cultural studies, because ultimately it was the shift toward the former that brought about the latter.

Stuart Hall has written much about the origins of cultural studies:

> From its inception, then, Cultural Studies was an "engaged" set of disciplines, addressing awkward but relevant issues about contemporary society and culture, often without benefit of that scholarly detachment or distance which the passage of time alone sometimes confers on other fields of study. The "contemporary"—which otherwise defined our terms of reference too narrowly—was, by definition, hot to handle. This tension (between what might loosely be called "political" and intellectual concerns) has shaped Cultural Studies ever since.[29]

It might be amusing to link this origin of "cultural studies" with Chateaubriand's text condemning all attempts at a history of the present, because of the overly strong passions in which the actor-chronicler is inevitably entangled. Stuart Hall's genealogical discussion suggests the very opposite. It doesn't matter who was the origin of what: we understand that the object is less important than the engagement of the one who is speaking. The contemporaneity of objects matters with regard to their role in shaking up fields of knowledge and practices. And above all, the contemporaneity of objects affects the commentator, caught up in the process of their existence. Cultural studies fully assumes the subjective implication of the theorist and its implication in the "dirty outside world." And besides, cultural studies is interested much less in objects than it is in practices. According to Raymond Williams, the true crisis in cultural theory, in our own time, is between this view of the work of art as an object and the alternative view of art as a practice.[30]

Now, an entirely new theory of context (and a profoundly contemporist one) is visible within cultural studies, an explicitly materialist theory. Instead of integrating the objects of study within an idealized historical continuity, or making them into simple reflections of historical contests and politics, it is a matter of interrogating their material conditions of production (both technical and institutional) and their social uses. The first works in this vein (those by Williams, Thompson, Hoggart), according to Stuart Hall, "inflected the term 'culture' away from its traditional moorings, getting behind the inert sense of 'period' which sustained the text/context distinction, moving the argument into the wider field of social practices and historical processes."[31] A less idealized but more concrete form of contemporaneity is unveiled with the observation of contemporary objects. And in fact, one of the fundamental distinctions arises from the abandonment of artifacts as privileged objects of culture for the study of processes and practices. In that sense, the principle of ranking, the canonization (which is nothing more than fetishization) proper to a vision centered on texts and artifacts, so important for sequentialist historicism, disappears in favor of an anthropological approach to cultural practices and forms of living. Now cultural practices, because they are above all relations, largely exceed texts and artistic artifacts. The "culture" of cultural studies, or rather, the "cultures," abandons the old distinctions important to aesthetics to seek out all the different forms of living (political, social, ideological, intimate...). Hall describes how the concept of culture itself became more democratized and less elite.[32]

One can find a lot written elsewhere about the Centre. Here I prefer to return to the focus of this book, because I perceive, as I approach its conclusion, that the history of cultural studies as Stuart Hall has traced it is pretty close to the scenario I spoke about in my introduction, the scenario on which I've continued to rely. This is the result of an epochal reflection; according to Hall, cultural studies "arose out of the debates over social and cultural changes in postwar Great Britain."[33] This is the great change from an old pyramidal structure to a new democratic, horizontal one. We ought to note that Raymond Williams and Richard Hoggart both came from the working class, while Stuart Hall was newly arrived from Jamaica. Even in their personal biographies, they typify that demographic reconfiguration in advanced societies that ended up giving an epochal sense to the word *contemporary*. But very soon a modal approach gave them the chance to inaugurate "a strikingly different kind of reflection on past and present"[34] and from there to envisage a modal signification for the contemporary. One of the oldest and strongest formulations of this came from Raymond Williams:

> We have then to see, first, as it were a temporal relation between a dominant culture and on the one hand a residual and on the other hand an emergent culture.[35]

An archaeology of the contemporary, then, becomes necessary, because modernist evolutionism presents itself as an ideological construction concealing the power relations between the dominant and the residual or the emergent. The present is marked by these three movements, and probably a great many others as well, so much so that culture never exists in the singular but is essentially plural. To describe and to engage with that horizontal plurality becomes the only viable ethical posture for a critic of the contemporary. To adopt that posture, we have to renounce the blinding exclusivity of objects and become attentive to processes, to materialities, to the forms of living. But not only that: there is also a practice, a methodology that one is always developing in the course of this inquiry. Stuart Hall writes,

> We claim, however, at least to know something of, and to have explored some of the problems consequent on, trying to develop new forms of collective intellectual practice. We know something of what this means as a practical condition of intellectual work. In this sense, we feel we have begun to anticipate some of the difficulties not of the past but of the future. No attempt should or could be made here to underestimate the tensions and contradictions produced by this mode of work. They are objective—in our situation—as well as subjective, and they are not to be resolved without costs. But they are at least "of our time": they belong to the present; they are not archaic, or merely inhabited and inherited out of academic habit.[36]

This inquiry has never ceased encountering, in artistic practices and in theoretical approaches, that form of collectivized work, that despecialization that shapes the contemporary mode of historical experience.

The birth of cultural studies in Great Britain has not been examined enough in its relation with the historical moment, especially the contemporary. This brief look shows very clearly that all the institutions we've encountered have given nearly obsessive attention to history conceived in terms of linearity. From the margins, but in a revolutionary way, cultural studies has mounted a wide-ranging institutional critique. The ruptures that cultural studies effected in objects of study, in both high and popular culture—these effects have been widely studied, but not enough attention has been paid to the fact that the Centre for Contemporary Cultural Studies's most powerful gesture of affirmation has less to do with the word "cultural" in the title and more with the implied word, "contemporary." It is probably as "contemporary studies" that "cultural studies" will continue to inspire us.

ON CONTEMPORISM

The inquiry nears its end, and its method has become clear. From one Foucault to a second one, if I may put it that way: from the Foucault of general history, the Foucault of dispersion, to the Foucault of heterotopia, the one who, in an era of the multiplication of simultaneities, proposed practicing spatial juxtaposition and montage rather than the discursive monologue. The more pervasive the presence of the contemporary, the more our awareness of the real becomes spatialized, and the less it inscribes itself into time. The contemporary is not the *terminus* of linear history but its contradiction. This idea of Foucault's was also, only slightly altered, that of Benjamin. But they remain, both of them, very much on the side of the minority—not discursively, but in practice. Certainly we all talk constantly about Foucault and Benjamin, but within the framework of orthodox history. People boast of their great heterodoxies within perfectly linear and monologic treatises. This is not the way to quit historicism. Contemporism, which is the inverse of historicism, asks us to depart from the same old path, to take another route. Such a departure can be observed most readily in the margins of history writing—for example, in certain exhibitions, among certain curator-theorists, adepts at montage and at counterwriting, to undo the linear, sequential, and successive representation of history. We can observe such intellectual movements in heterodox historians whose work seems to hesitate between theoretical writing and artistic production. We observe them in the work of the founders of cultural studies, thanks to whom the contemporary has become a mode of perceiving the real. We observe them, finally, in a representation of time that is much more archaeological than historical, in which the present, a multidirectional time, is the sole path of access to historical consciousness. This counterwriting is, again, perfectly in phase with the representation of the contemporary that is emerging, on one side, from non-Western narrations and, on the other, from the proliferation of mediatized temporalities. A coherence arises out of all this: contemporism opposes historicism, and it suggests another strategy for dealing with historical time, one that gives life to other representational practices and other cultural significations. It has furnished the logic of my inquiry.

CONCLUSION

Locations of the Contemporary

One can make a talisman out of multiplicity all one likes and try to give the same amount of attention to all the givens that present themselves—and indeed, these two conditions form the contemporist ethic—but one remains fetishist nonetheless, almost involuntarily, tempted by the unity of an authority that would explain everything about the experience of the world and its writing. Emmanuelle Pireyre's work concerning "documentary fictions" has played a significant role in this book, from its introduction to its conclusion. In the introduction, where I worked through the most problematic signification of the contemporary, it was Pireyre who spoke of a "commerce with time." And her work is present in the conclusion, because this *ars poetica* seems to me to be a model for contemporary theory writing:

> On the one hand, the world makes such a loud noise, and makes it so well that it pours ideas down into us like a rainstorm, but on the other hand these thousands of ideas are not given to us in a pure, accessible state, but rather as if packaged; and unwrapping them constitutes a good part of our writing lives.[1]

The experience of the world is that of brouhaha. Writing, according to Emmanuelle Pireyre, is partly confronting this brouhaha (welcoming it, listening to it) and partly "unwrapping packages," defetishizing it. She thus draws an opposition between documentary writing and what we usually call the novel, which she holds at arm's length:

> Hypothesis: that the narrative thread proper to the novel, the part we like about novels, always tends more toward the movie screen and the darkness of the theater than it does toward the computer; and that even in the case of a badly handled narrative and even in the case of creative nonfiction such as memoir, there is a division between the real and the fictional, a plunging into fiction, an envelope of obscurity that separates and protects fiction from the existence of the author and that of the reader. So, the books I want to speak about intervene and make their commentary during the show itself; they are written and read with the light on and not in semi-isolation—whether the latter is a synonym for freedom or peril.[2]

Some years ago now, I pushed the button "contemporary," and a "rainstorm of ideas" came pouring down into my mind. I could have ignored them, acted as if they did not exist, and turned my gaze to Giorgio Agamben's cinema screen. I could have (if I'd had the means to do so) constructed a fiction that would have insisted on its rightness, saying, look, I'm telling you, this is the contemporary and nothing else. But I preferred to take the time to "unwrap the packages" and "make my commentary during the show itself." In that sense—and I say this very guardedly, and with no intention of burnishing any pretentions I might have as to artistic nobility—in my view, this book comes closer to those documentary fictions, the ones Emmanuelle Pireyre describes, or those curatorial activities I've described, than to the majority of essays published in the human sciences.

Nevertheless, even if it was impossible to produce a unified fiction, there is a single dynamic, a single movement, that can be seen at every location explored throughout the journey and inquiry of this book. They could be described like this: the modern framework is flooded by a multiplicity that it cannot contain and that shows it up for what it really is—an imaginary, an illusion, an imaginary of distinction and of separation, whereas the contemporary, for its part, offers us an imaginary of nondistinction.

HISTORICITY/ARCHAEOLOGY

Let's go back: the contemporary is perhaps, above all (but not quite above all), a question posed to (or maybe by) historicity. And not to (or maybe by) history. Our first reflex is to think that the name "contemporary" signals a historical identity, that is, a moment in which aesthetic, political, and historical experience all crystallize in a word that, like the categories with which it is in dialogue ("ancient," "early," "Renaissance," "modern," "modernity"), has to do with temporality. From that reflex, one could deduce that, like those others, the word signals a moment of great intensity in historical awareness of the present. But no category of historical identity has ever been so globalized, so generalized, so spread among the masses.

But far from coming to enrich the list of historical-aesthetic categories, the contemporary signals the abandonment of a linear, sequential, successive, and euchronic representation of history, and it signals the abandonment of the demarcation between past and present, those two parameters that underpin modern historical representation. When I say abandon, I imply at times a contempt for, at others a critique of, at others an extremely violent rejection of, that separation as a mode of historical being. This abandonment is not precisely dateable, localizable, or attributable; on the contrary, it is—and this only makes it more spectacular—diffused, contradictory, massive. The contemporary is thus a matter of a semantization of historical times. It signals as much a transformation of individual and collective perceptions of the present (the relationship to the past is much less analytical and much more inclusive) as it does a transformation of critical modes (from the mainline European–United States historiography to the non-Western modes developed especially by postcolonial theory to heterodox histories) and a transformation of artistic representations, very much obsessed with the superimposition of historical temporalities.

In this sense, the contemporary may best be considered as the cancellation of the modernist hypothesis about historicity, which represented time as an irreversible succession of sequences. Contemporary theories and representations of history show in the strongest way that every reality, every object, is traversed by multiple times. Contrary to what one might think, the success of the word *contemporary* owes a lot to the awareness that anachronism (and not euchronism)—that is, the superimposition of apparently contradictory, distinct, and homogeneous temporalities—is the other name of contemporaneity, understood as a co-temporality. In what is only apparently a paradox, the result of this approach is the valorization of the present as the sole historical time. "There is no history except that *which follows the current present*"[3] could be the slogan for the contemporary. True, but only if we charge that current present with all temporalities. In this sense, *present* and *presentism* are words too weak to stand for this contemporaneization of all times within the present. The past does not exist, being perceptible only in the traces of it still carried by the present: this is what *contemporary* means in thinking about history. It signals that a "historical" model concurrent with the modern hypothesis is slowly beginning to substitute itself for it. This model, with the memory of the past lodging itself in the materiality of the present, can be called archaeological. So it is no surprise to see archaeology becoming the totemic concept of the present, and another name for contemporism, the study of the contemporary.

Once we understand it in this way, the contemporary is no longer really a historical category that follows the modern, whether in the form of an antimodernity or that of a postmodernity (both deploy the same dynamic). It is no longer simply a period; rather, it is a moment that critiques periodization. It is a mode of being in historical time, one that indicates that, if "we have never been modern," we have certainly always been contemporaries.

TIME AND MEDIA

In this sense, it is a temporal business and therefore a political question. I side with the hypothesis of the historian Benedict Anderson, who thought we could distinguish community forms in terms of their conception of co-temporality. Contemporaneity forms communities. To have the sensation of sharing the same time is a necessary precondition to the feeling of belonging together. Thus there is a relation between the form of community and the type of contemporaneity, each being invested by political discourse. One of modernity's most remarkable traits was the way it constituted communities without physical co-presence. From the moment that the sensation of being part of a common body is produced without physically being in the same area, that sensation is essentially media based and mediatized. So there is a very strong relation between the technological imaginary, forms of political subjectivity, and the relationship to contemporaneity. Benedict Anderson showed how the national imaginary was linked to the rise of the novel and the spread of printing. Following up on his work, the anthropologist Arjun Appadurai analyzed how supranational communities, in particular diasporic communities, were formed by means of new technologies of simultaneity (audio and video recordings). I've envisaged a third form of contemporaneity, linked to the hyper-mediatized world, multiplying temporalities themselves, articulating diverse forms of simultaneity. This last form of contemporaneity corresponds to the globalized imaginary.

These three media-based imaginaries coexist, because the appearance of new media (and, with them, new political imaginaries for sharing the same time together) does not lead to the

disappearance of the old. The contemporaneity of the hypermediatized era comprises many media-based imaginaries that correspond to political communities: local, national, supranational,
global. Each medium setting out a temporality appropriate to
co-presence, these temporalities begin to superimpose upon each
other. The information and communication technologies that
possess all the temporal qualities of contemporaneity (simultaneity, synchronicity, polychronicity) reinforce this temporal com-
plexity. This is so much the case that the contemporary experience of time feels more like a concordance of temporalities than
a single time, a concordance that is also more subjective than
collective: it's not postulating that a single unique, unified present
is shared by the community but rather that what the community shares is a subjectivized polychronicity. Multiplicity comes to
dominate unity.

The contemporary speaks of this experience of time, and this
explains why our capacity for attention is at the heart of current
debates. If there are some (like Nicholas Carr) who ask whether
our "literary brain," previously capable of maintaining a prolonged
state of attention (a "hyperattention"), was not now being replaced
by a multiattentional faculty, there are others (like Yves Citton) who
outline an ecology of attention, one far less dialectic, one where
the awareness of co-temporality—that is, the superimposition of
polytemporal experiences (and this already describes the experience of reading)—has become a central issue. What time are we
living in? This is perhaps the question that has most haunted this
essay. To be contemporary, one might say, is to have the experience of that simultaneity of attentional solicitations. Of course,
this is no real novelty. But it is probably in our moment that this
has become our principal, decisive experience. Because thinking
about this mode of being in time has led us to bring up the subject
of literature, it seems to me that this contemporaneity, far from
spelling the end of reading, has a tendency to valorize exactly those
interstice or vacuole forms, those temporal compositions, that are

often aesthetic constructions. No doubt, this is a resource to explore to better understand contemporary literary and artistic practices.

Historicity, archaeology, the mediatized experience of time: a single conceptual line running through these becomes visible so that the contemporary signifies the end of a sequential and successive representation of time and turns instead to a superimposition of temporalities. And at this point, we are moving ever further from the modern hypothesis.

A VERY LARGE NUMBER

These transformations in historical awareness and temporal perception can only be explained by means of a new actualization of the multiplicity of subjects who experience it. Numbers, very large numbers, have preoccupied societies since modernity. Modern societies disciplined large numbers into concepts: crowds, classes, peoples, communities. These concepts in turn produce hierarchies: hierarchies of discourse, of social positions, of regions. But these concepts collapse under the double pressure of massification and differentiation. Logically, the great massification that followed the Second World War produced a new historical identifier: the contemporary. This massification, linked to demographic change, has not ceased since then, has in fact globalized, with all the imperfections we know so well. We have surely passed from the large number to the very large number. And the very large number is not the same thing as the large number was. A single political concept has emerged to take account of the phenomenon: that of the multitude. I've suggested distinguishing the pair modernity–community from another pair: contemporary–multitude. Unlike other forms of modern assemblies, the multitude is not reducible to a unity but instead is performative and temporary. It can be recognized by its auto-organization as well as by its principles of heterogeneity and multiplicity. It entails processes of dehierarchization, horizontalization, and deauthorization, processes that my inquiry has attempted to show are present in everything from a fanzine to a book of philosophy.

The very large number, the multitude—this is not only a political question. It entails an imaginary as well as forms of thought and methods. The media theorist Lev Manovich explained in a radio interview that the Web, structured by hypertext and databases, has brought about a dehierarchization and a coexistence of disparate elements. Linking a photo to a text, an image to a video, an article to a book, is to select out of potentially infinite data points rather than using established genres to produce a kind of thought that will connect to the multitude and favor the very large number. But, inversely, these kinds of thought would perhaps never have seen the light of day if they hadn't been structured by the multitude and the very large number. The Internet is not a library. The library treats the very large number by hierarchization, whereas the Internet treats it by horizontalization into a supple structure, one that is always beginning all over again.

And the world is no longer structured like a library, as we used to believe. We still seek what its imaginary is, as it changes from year to year. These days, it seems as if the world is (de)structured like "big data." As one proof of this, my venerable discipline, literary studies, so deeply attached to the library, has also become infatuated with this new fetish—though with limited results, we must admit. The fetish of big data is simply the incarnation of the new fact so well analyzed by Bruno Latour:

> Modern temporality gave the impression of a continuous acceleration, rejecting the past of more and more masses of the human and nonhuman alike. Irreversibility has changed sides. If there is one thing we can no longer get rid of, it is those natures and multitudes, both equally global.[4]

Both share the same time.

THE SPATIAL TURN

Moving from time to space, we again encounter Foucault, who said that his current epoch was that of space, while at the same time being the epoch of simultaneity, of juxtaposition, and of dispersion:

> We are at a moment, I believe, when our experience of the world is less that of a long life developing through time than that of a network that connects points and intersects with its own skein.[5]

Linking simultaneity, juxtaposition, and, thus, spatiality, this text, already an old one, is incredibly visionary, almost prophetic; writing almost at the origin of the whole movement, Foucault can see the premises so clearly. This originating movement is one we have already called the spatial turn in thought (and, at the same time, the spatial turn in artistic practices). There is a logic present here. The critique of historicism, of history, and of modern temporality— all these go along with a valorization of spatiality in all forms of thought and with the representation of spatiality (notably, geographical representation). In any case, this geocritique[6] is entirely in accord with the diffuse and sometimes contradictory ensemble of thought we call postcolonial. We can begin to understand why we have not found anything better than a spatial concept to stand for our historical moment: it is globalization that has in large part placed our time in a dialectical relationship with modernity. From modernity to globalization first of all involves a complete change in the hermeneutic mode—from thinking in time to thinking in space. This is the spatial turn. This is what allows us to account for a multiplicity of concurrent histories or simply parallel ones that coexist and are in juxtaposition. The spatial turn is, simply, thinking the multitude in a dehierarchized manner.

PUBLIC SPACES AND CANONS

Closely related to this spatial turn is the essential question of public spaces. The multidisciplinarity of the question is one of the reasons it is so essential. But there is more. While the issue of public spaces is one of the rare transhistoric issues, for some fifty years now, it has been explicitly or implicitly at the heart of our great theoretical debates. We must recognize Habermas, who first raised the question and thus made the question of contemporaneity central to our modern political systems—a contemporaneity founded upon debate and participation within a common public sphere. But Habermas overidealized the modern public sphere, allowing it only one incarnation within the bourgeois public sphere in its movement toward rationality. Nancy Fraser's critical rereading of the public sphere gives us an invaluable tool for understanding contemporaneity. Fraser points out that this idealized public sphere assumes a great many exclusions, the most important of which is gender, but there are other exclusions based on property and on race—inequalities of gender, class, and ethnicity. Far from idealizing a single public sphere, she proposes that we think of society as a kind of arena, but an agonistic one consisting of a multitude of publics and counterpublics, both performative and temporary. I've seen the truth of this representation throughout my study, within the theoretical, the cultural, and the political universes. To conceive of the contemporary is to recognize at once that there are multitudes of public spaces, temporary and coexisting. In any case, this is how I have chosen to study contemporary literature, which is not limited to the book or to an idealized public sphere. The literary, instead, seems like an arena of debate, where the public sphere enters into dialogue with a multitude of public spaces and deploys expressions entirely outside the editorial circuit. Literature is only one example, but it is an emblematic one to the extent that literature has been one of the key concepts of modernity, just as publication is in the process of becoming one of the key concepts of the contemporary. But all other contemporary cultural phenomena can be and should be studied using the theory of public spaces.

This representation of cultural objects signals the end of the canonical approach, which had been so determinative in the past. Or, more precisely, it signals the end of the approach that assumes a unique, essentialist, naturalized canon. Recognizing and describing the multitude of canons as well as the process of canonization are thus preconditions for every critical study of the contemporary—and also for every contemporary critical activity.

CONTROVERSIES AND GLOBALISM

Controversy thus becomes the modality for constructing the meaning of the epoch. In itself, this is nothing new: meaning can only emerge from conflict. But what is undoubtedly new is, on one hand, recognizing the preeminence of controversy and, on the other, recognizing that these controversies always have the same spatial dynamic, that is (and I grant the banality of the affirmation), that they have been globalized. Among those that I have discussed, the three that stand out most clearly are (1) the debate over the *post-*, (2) the controversy over absolute culture, and (3) the contemporary in the critique of art.

The crowd of *posts* (postmodernism, postcolonialism, postfeminism, etc.) is interesting to observe because it fits well with the choice of *contemporary* as our key word. But these *posts* are anything but homogeneous; on the contrary, we can detect a movement of dissociation among the various *posts* and, beyond that, a distancing from the use of *post-* as a historical identifier, which seems to prolong the centrality of the modern narrative. The word *contemporary* deconstructs that narrative, showing it to be exactly that. The *post-* and related terms (the after, survivals, the beyond, melancholy) have all come to be seen by many thinkers as provincial, related to the "Western."

The same kind of movement was evident in our examination of the critique of art calling itself into question over the contemporary. Closely allied with the old center of modernity (New York), critique was unable to extricate itself from the academic world (or ghetto) or from metatheoretical debate and the effects of its discourse. It was reborn in a new center, Berlin, which was not in fact a center (in the sense of a cultural capital), but it stumbled over one of the major controversies of the epoch in Europe: that of the cultural absolute. That controversy was ignored by the Asian theoretical axis of New Delhi and Hong Kong, which freed itself from melancholic historical visions and took up the theoretical reflection on the contemporary without ending up mired, as had so often happened, in an impasse of negativity. The critical platform (the Asian Art Archive) developed there was launched to "document the multiple recent histories of the contemporary in the region." With only a slight variation, I could adopt that as my own goal, because I have tried to document, in a way, some of the multiple recent histories of the contemporary within the world. Documenting histories is not the same thing as constructing a narrative, because the latter always seeks to produce a homogeneous epoch, no matter what it costs. The heart of my inquiry, somewhat like a mirror of the Asian Art Archive, is the constitution of an archive whose principal objective is to collect, to connect, to make heard, and to show—all operations that, by structuring the field of the visible, also have a political dimension.

In this sense, the contemporary is not simply a word nor simply a concept but a hermeneutic tool. The moment we reject the linear and sequential model of historicism in favor of an archaeological and contemporist one, we reject what used to be our mode of interpretation and of exposition; we reject continuity to privilege discontinuity, superimposition, and montage.

DISPLAYING THE CONTEMPORARIES

These few central ideas, these points of tension, I now see, will interest me henceforth as much as the signifier "contemporary." Its plasticity, both in geographic and disciplinary terms, its untranslatability, made it at first a concept difficult to grasp, contradictory. But once going beyond historicist representation and moving to archaeological ones, conceiving a polychronic and noneuchronic temporality, rejecting the idealized public sphere in favor of a multiplicity of public spaces, and decentering and polycentering our geography to welcome the very large number—then all these parameters constitute a discernible historical identity. The contemporary is indeed that connected multiplicity that lifts the modern hypothesis off temporality. Does it merit becoming a noun, substantivation? Do we really need a unifying historical concept? I believe we do, even though saying that seems to reveal the modern deformation of thought. It echoes our old belief in the homogeneity of epochs, because modern thought was born in a more homogeneous world than today's is. But of course, sometimes all one has to rely on are the old reflexes. Using them is necessary to get beyond them. To conceive of the contemporary is to be done with the idea that there is *one* sole object to conceive of. Instead, there are multiple realities to reveal.

This assumes that one is situated at the heart of the machine and not observing it from the outside—that one is working and engaging with the machine, in order to think about it.

Acknowledgments

The general structure of this inquiry was first presented under the title "What Is the Contemporary? Brief Archaeology of a Question," in *Revista de Estudios Hispánicos* 48, no. 1 (March 2014), in a translation by Lily Robert-Foley. The notion of "brouhaha" was first introduced in the article "Zum-zum-zum: estudo sobre o nome contemporâneo," translated by Marcos Flamínio Peres and published in the Brazilian journal *Celeuma*, no. 4 (May 2014). The section on the public spaces of contemporary literature was the object of a first version translated by Matthew H. Evans under the title "The Public Spaces of Contemporary Literature," published in the journal *Qui Parle: Critical Humanities and Social Sciences* 22, no. 2 (Spring–Summer 2014); in a Spanish translation by Martín Arias ("Los espacios públicos de la literature contemporánea"), it appeared in the journal *Cuadernos Lirico,* no. 13 (2015). The first chapter of the book was sketched out in the article "Displaying the Contemporary/The Contemporary on Display," published in the Scottish journal *The Drouth,* no. 52 (Summer 2015). I had the honor and the pleasure of presenting some of the themes in this book under the auspices of the Leverhulme Lectures that I gave in spring 2015 at the University of St. Andrews.

Beyond these publications, the conception and the drafting

of this book have been enriched by a number of friends and colleagues who freely gave of their time to read and discuss my ideas. Here I want to thank particularly Emily Apter, Martín Arias, Bruno Blanckeman, Odile Cazenave, Yves Citton, Jérôme David, Jérôme Game, Bertrand Gervais, Héctor Hoyos, Margaret-Anne Hutton, Aliocha Imhoff, Claire Joubert, Julio Premat, Kantuta Quiros, Zahia Rahmani, Johnny Rodger, and Ravi Sundaram. I wish also to thank the Leverhulme Trust for their funding of the Leverhulme Network for Contemporary Studies. More generally, I have worked for these last years in the department of the Masters de Création Littéraire in the University of Paris 8. My constant exchanges there with colleagues and students have certainly influenced this book.

Jean-Max Colard, François Cusset, Olivia Rosenthal, and Tiphaine Samoyault have played a crucial role in reading the first version of this essay and in finding the right phrases to encourage me to continue and, sometimes, to reorient my work. David Ruffel read and corrected the final version after having accompanied me on every step of the inquiry. I thank all five of them for their support, their friendship, and their generosity.

Finally, I dedicate this book to Ninon, and I offer it to May, Max, and Misha. In the brouhaha of the worlds.

Notes

INTRODUCTION

1 *Contemporâneo Hoje* (São Paulo: Edições Anteriores, 2013), http://www.mariantonia.prceu.usp.br/celeuma/?q=edicoes -anteriores.

2 Hans Robert Jauss, "Modernity and Literary Tradition," trans. Christian Thorne, *Critical Inquiry* 31 (Winter 2005): 329–64.

3 For a detailed study of the lexical uses of *contemporary*, and more generally on the aesthetic hypothesis, see Lionel Ruffel, ed., *Qu'est-ce que le contemporain?* (Nantes: Éditions Cécile Defaut, 2010).

4 I make use here of Vincent Descombes's categories (see his "Qu'est-ce qu'être contemporain?," in *Le Genre humain* 35 [February 2000]: 20–33) with some inflections of my own. Descombes writes, "From the philosophers' point of view, there are at least two major conceptions of the contemporary possible. The first comes from the philosophy of history. We see it in those history programs that include toward the end the study of the modern and the contemporary epoch, with the 'contemporary world' being presented as the most advanced point of the 'modern world.' . . . In the epochal conception, the contemporary is treated like a fellow citizen with the epoch: just as compatriots are from the same country, so contemporaries are from the

same historical period.... The second conception comes from reflecting on the philosophy of time. If one asks for an idea of the contemporary from the philosophy of time, the contemporary will be conceived as a kind of struggle among many current transformations. Now, the concept of the current is a modal one; the current is defined by contrast with the potential or the possible.... The current is above all *not* what we find in the newspapers; rather, it is what is effectively being produced, it is that which is in the process of affecting us, even if the newspapers choose not to speak of this. Given the role that the idea of the current plays in this second conception of the contemporary, one might speak of a *modal* comprehension, as opposed to an epochal one" (20).

I make use of these ideas while simplifying them. The *epochal* conception designates the approaches that insist on our historical time and what distinguishes it from others. The *modal* conception is seen as a certain relationship between history and the current.

5   Reinhardt Koselleck, *Futures Past: On the Semantics of Historical Time,* trans. Keith Tribe (New York: Columbia University Press, 2004).

6   François Hartog, *Regimes of Historicity: Presentism and Experiences of Time,* trans. Saskia Brown (New York: Columbia University Press, 2015).

7   Ibid., 18.

8   See Boris Groys, "Comrades of Time," *e-flux Journal* 11 (December 2009).

9   Emmanuelle Pireyre, "Fictions documentaires," in *Devenirs du roman,* ed. François Bégaudeau (Paris: Inculte, 2007), 124–25. Italics mine.

10   Ibid., 128.

11   Ibid., 137.

12   Roberto Saviano, *Gomorrah: A Personal Journey into the Violent International Empire of Naples' Organized Crime System,* trans. Virginia Jewiss (New York: Picador, 2007), 211–12.

13 English in the original.—Trans.

14 See David Ruffel, "Une littérature contextuelle," *Littérature* 60 (April 2010): 61–73.

15 Bruno Latour, "An Attempt at a 'Compositionist Manifesto,'" *New Literary History* 41, no. 3 (2010): 471–90.

16 Ibid., 484.

17 See Dominique Quessada, *L'Inséparé: Essai sur le monde sans Autre* (Paris: Presses Universitaires de France, 2013).

18 Bruno Latour, *We Have Never Been Modern,* trans. Catherine Porter (Cambridge, Mass.: Harvard University Press, 1993).

19 Ibid., 10.

20 Jauss, "Modernity and Literary Tradition," 332.

21 Ibid., 333.

22 Ibid., 341.

23 Ibid., 363.

24 Ibid.

25 Latour, *We Have Never Been Modern,* 69.

26 Ibid.

27 Ibid., 47.

28 Ibid., 77.

29 Giorgio Agamben, "What Is the Contemporary?," in *What Is an Apparatus?,* trans. David Kishik and Stefan Pedatella, 39–54 (Stanford, Calif.: Stanford University Press, 2009).

FIRST SERIES: EXPOSITION

1 See Jesús Pedro Lorente, *Les Musées d'art moderne et contemporain: Une exploration conceptuelle et historique,* trans. J. Bastoen (Paris: L'Harmattan, 2008), 332.

2 On this issue, see again ibid.

3 James S. Plaut and Nelson Aldrich, *"Modern Art" and the American Public* (Boston: Institute of Contemporary Art, 1948), https://ia800509.us.archive.org/24/items/modernartamerica00inst/modernartamerica00inst.pdf.

4 See Serge Guilbaut, *Comment New York vola l'idée d'art moderne*

(1983; repr., Paris: Hachette littératures, "Pluriel," 2006).

5   Reprinted in Serge Guilbaut, ed., *Be-Bomb: The Transatlantic War of Images and All That Jazz* (Barcelona: MACBA, 2007).

6   From Clement Greenberg, the highly influential post–World War II art critic, who defended the idea of a purity in each artistic practice, a deliberate concentration so as to explore the particular medium being used.

7   See Brian O'Doherty, *Inside the White Cube: The Ideology of Gallery Space* (Berkeley: University of California Press, 1999).

8   According to Jeebesh Bagchi, between 1987 and 2007, the number of museums in the world grew by 90 percent (without counting galleries, biennales, and temporary exhibition spaces). See *Field Notes 01: The And: An Expanded Questionnaire on the Contemporary* (Hong Kong: Asian Art Archive, 2012), https://issuu.com/asiaartarchivehk/docs/FN01_the_and_eng.

9   O'Doherty, *Inside the White Cube*, 38.

10 "Walter Benjamin: Mondrian 1963–1986" at the International Exhibition of Modern Art, Armory Show, New York, 2013, a lecture in which Goran Djordjevic plays the role of Walter Benjamin speaking about the works of Piet Mondrian. This lecture can be seen in its entirety at https://vimeo.com/55504143; further references to it will be attributed to "the speaker."—Trans.

11 Jeff Khonsary, ed., *Walter Benjamin: Recent Writings* (Vancouver: New Documents, 2014).

12 "Art is defined by the narrative of the history of art, and it only exists within that history," said the conference speaker.

13 The conference speaker, never stingy with shocking phrases and provocations, concludes thus: "To be an artist in our day is like being a priest at the moment of the appearance of natural philosophy: an obsolete class." He also says, "Museums will exist so that visitors can come to them the way non-believers come to the cathedrals: to see what art was, and what the museum was. Most art museums will become museums of art."

14 O'Doherty, *Inside the White Cube*, 14.

15 Ibid., 15.

16   Ibid., 24.

17   Ibid., 16.

18   Patricia Falguières, French introduction to O'Doherty's *White Cube,* 9.

19   Philippe Vasset, *Bandes alternées* (Paris: Fayard, 2006), 9.

20   Douglas Crimp, *On the Museum's Ruins* (Cambridge, Mass.: MIT Press, 1993).

21   Michael Hardt and Antonio Negri, *Multitude: War and Democracy in the Age of Empire* (New York: Penguin, 2005).

22   Antonio Negri, "Contemporaneity between Modernity and Postmodernity," in *Antimonies of Art and Culture: Modernity, Postmodernity, Contemporaneity,* ed. Nancy Condee, Okwui Enwezor, and Terry Smith, 23–29 (Durham, N.C.: Duke University Press, 2008).

23   It is no coincidence that two of the most passionate publications devoted to contemporary culture and politics in France today are titled *Multitudes* (Hubbub) and *Vacarme* (Racket).

SECOND SERIES: MEDIA

1   "ENSAN no doubt has neither the visibility nor the notoriety of the great benchmark universities and schools. This fact encourages a more uninhibited inquiry and even, dare one say, a deeper one, as local contributions to a culture can be more constructive than those arising from more global ones." Emmanuel Doutriaux and Arnaud François, eds., *Qu'est-ce que le contemporain?* (Montpellier: de l'Espérou, "Cahiers de l'École nationale supérierure d'architecture de Normandie," 2007), 13.

2   Robert Venturi, Steven Izenour, and Denise Scott Brown, *Learning from Las Vegas* (Cambridge, Mass.: MIT Press, 1977).

3   Charles Jencks, *The Language of Postmodern Architecture,* rev. ed. (New York: Rizzoli, 1977).

4   Frederic Jameson, *Postmodernism, or The Cultural Logic of Late Capitalism* (Durham, N.C.: Duke University Press, 1992).

5   Ibid., 19.

6   Ibid., 14.

7   Pireyre, "Fictions documentaires," 124.

8   Doutriaux and François, *Qu'est-ce que le contemporain?*, 27.

9   Ibid., 29.

10 Georges Didi-Huberman, *Devant le temps: Histoire de l'art et anachronisme des images* (Paris: Minuit "Critique," 2000), 16.

11 Benedict Anderson, *Imagined Communities: Reflections on the Origin and Spread of Nationalism,* rev ed. (New York: Verso, 2006), 25n34.

12 Ibid., 37.

13 Ibid., 38.

14 Arjun Appadurai, *Modernity at Large: Cultural Dimensions of Globalization* (Minneapolis: University of Minnesota Press, 1996).

15 Ibid., 4.

16 Nicolas Carr, "Is Google Making Us Stupid?," *The Atlantic,* July/August 2008, https://www.theatlantic.com/magazine /archive/2008/07/is-google-making-us-stupid/306868/.

17 Yves Citton, *The Ecology of Attention* (Cambridge: Polity, 2017).

18 Ibid., 19.

19 Walter Benjamin, "Little History of Photography," in *The Work of Art in the Age of Its Technological Reproducibility and Other Writings on Media,* ed. Michael William Jennings, 274–98 (Cambridge, Mass.: Harvard University Press, 2008), and Benjamin, "Reflections on Radio," ibid., 391–92. See also the study by Philippe Baudouin, *Au microphone, Dr. Walter Benjamin: Walter Benjamin et la creation radiophonique, 1929–1933* (Paris: Maison des sciences de l'homme, "Phila," 2009).

20 Jussi Parikka, *What Is Media Archaelogy?* (Cambridge: Polity, 2012).

21 Of course, media archaeology will relativize that birth, finding that the cinematographic experience had had precedents in visual culture and literature. See Daniel Banda and José Moure, *Avant le cinema: L'oeil et l'image* (Paris: Armand Colin, 2012).

22 See Daniel Banda and José Moure, *Le Cinéma: Naissance*

d'un art, 1895–1920 (Paris: Flammarion, "Champs," 2008), 34.

23 The phrase alludes to the subtitle of the book by Siegfried Zielinski, *Archäologie der Medien: Zur Tiefenzeit des technischen Hörens und Sehens* (Reinbek bei Hamburg: Rowohlt, 2002).

24 Walter Benjamin, "The Work of Art in the Age of Its Technological Reproducibility," 2nd version, in Benjamin, *Work of Art,* 20–21.

25 See Chantal Mouffe, *Le Politique et ses enjeux: Pour une démocratie plurielle* (Paris: La Découverte-MAUSS, 1994).

26 Jacques Derrida, *Specters of Marx: The State of the Debt, the Work of Mourning, and the New International,* trans. Peggy Kamuf (New York: Routledge, 2006).

27 Pireyre, "Fictions documentaires," 137.

THIRD SERIES: PUBLICATION

1 Gilles Deleuze and Félix Guattari, *What Is Philosophy?*, trans. Hugh Tomlinson and Graham Burchill (New York: Verso, 1994).

2 I must point out that only the Italian and French publishers agreed as to the book's exceptional status. In the English edition, "What Is the Contemporary?" is relegated to the status of an "other essay." Giorgio Agamben, *"What Is an Apparatus?" and Other Essays,* trans. D. Kishik and S. Pedatella (Stanford, Calif.: Stanford University Press, 2009). So it is with the Spanish version as well: "¿Que es lo contemporáneo?" is merely one of the pieces collected under the title *Desnudez,* trans. M. Ruvituso, M. T. D'Meza, and C. Sardoy (Buenos Aires: Adriana Hidalgo, 2011).

3 Giorgio Agamben, "What Is the Contemporary?," in *What Is an Apparatus?,* 40.

4 Ibid., 45.

5 Ibid., 41.

6 Ibid., 40.

7 Ibid., 39–40.

8 Ibid., 41.

9   Vincent Descombes, "Qu'est-ce qu'être contemporain?," *Le Genre humain,* no. 35 (Winter 1999–Spring 2000), reprinted in *Le Raisonnement de l'ours et autres essais de philosophie pratique* (Paris: Seuil, "La couleur des idées," 2007), 22–23.

10 Chateaubriand, *Mémoires d'outre-tombe,* book 33, chapter 9, ed. P. Clarac (Paris: Le Livre de poche, 1973), 3:249–50.

11 Agamben, "What Is the Contemporary?," 44.

12 Descombes, "Qu'est-ce qu'être contemporain?," 24.

13 Alain Badiou, *Le Siècle* (Paris: Seuil, 2005), translated by Alberto Toscano as *The Century* (Cambridge: Polity Press, 2007). Badiou's extensive discussion of Mandelstam's poem "The Age" begins on p. 11.—Trans.

14 Agamben, "What Is the Contemporary?," 42.

15 Ibid., 44.

16 Jean-Marie Schaeffer, *Petite écologie des études littéraires: Pourquoi et comment étudier la littérature?* (Vincennes: Thierry Marchaisse, 2011), 12.

17 Agamben, "What Is the Contemporary?," 45.

18 Ibid., 46.

19 Olivia Rosenthal and Lionel Ruffel, "Introduction," *Littérature,* no. 160 (2010), http://www.cairn.info/revue-litterature -2010-4-page-3.htm.

20 The e-magazine *Chaoïd, creation-critique* published eleven issues between 2000 and 2007, bringing together literature, the arts, theory, and experimentation. It also organized interdisciplinary exhibitions.

21 Ibid.

22 Jürgen Habermas, *L'Espace public: Archéologie de la publicité comme dimension constitutive de la société bourgeoise,* trans. M. B. de Launay (1962; repr., Paris: Payot, "Critique de la politique," 1993). The book was translated into English by Thomas Burger, with the assistance of Frederick Lawrence, as *The Structural Transformation of the Public Sphere: An Inquiry into a Category of Bourgeois Society* (Cambridge, Mass.: MIT Press, 1991).

23 Ibid., 32.

24 Ibid,., 43.

25 Nancy Fraser, "Rethinking the Public Sphere: A Contribution to the Critique of Actually Existing Democracy," *Social Text* 25/26 (1990): 60–61.

26 Ibid., 61.

27 Ibid., 62.

28 Richard Hoggart, *The Uses of Literacy: Aspects of Working-Class Life* (London: Chatto and Windus, 1957); Jacques Rancière, *Proletarian Nights* (London: Verso, 2012); Lawrence Levine, *Highbrow/Lowbrow: The Emergence of Cultural Hierarchy in America* (Cambridge, Mass.: Harvard University Press, 1990).

29 Gil-Scot Heron, *The Vulture,* reprint ed. (1970; repr., New York: Grove Press, 2013), was translated into French as *Le Vautour* by J.-F. Ménard (Paris: L'Olivier, "Soul Fiction," 1998). The other early novel was *The Nigger Factory* (1972; repr., Edinburgh: Canongate, 2010).

30 See the introduction to the volume edited by Gisèle Sapiro, *Les Contradictions de la globalization éditoriale* [The contradictions of globalized publishing] (Paris: Nouveau Monde, 2009). See also André Schiffrin, *The Business of Books: How the International Conglomerates Took Over Publishing and Changed the Way We Read* (London: Verso, 2000). And see also Françoise Benhamou, *L'Économie de la culture* (Paris: La Découverte, "Repères," 1996).

31 See Mark McGurl, *The Program Era: Postwar Fiction and the Rise of Creative Writing* (Cambridge, Mass.: Harvard University Press, 2009).

32 See esp. Pierre Bourdieu, *Rules of Art: Genesis and Structure of the Literary Field,* trans. Susan Emanuel (Stanford, Calif.: Stanford University Press, 1996).

33 See http://www.encyclopediedelaparole.org/.

FOURTH SERIES: CONTROVERSY

1   Jean-François Lyotard, "Réponse à la question: qu'est-ce que le post-modern?," *Critique* 419 (1982): 357–67.

2   Hal Foster, *The Return of the Real: Art and Theory at the End of the Century* (Cambridge, Mass.: MIT Press, 1996), 204.

3   Donna Haraway, "A Cyborg Manifesto: Science, Technology, and Socialist-Feminism in the Late 20th Century," reprinted in *Simians, Cyborgs, and Women,* 149–82 (New York: Routledge, 1990).

4   For more on Spivak's "subalterns," see *Can the Subaltern Speak? Reflections on the History of an Idea,* ed. Rosemary Morris (New York: Columbia University Press, 2010), which contains a revised and recently republished edition of Spivak's well-known essay from the "History" chapter of her much larger, major work *Critique of Postcolonial Reason: Toward a History of the Vanishing Present* (Cambridge, Mass.: Harvard University Press, 1999).

5   Ngugi wah Thiong'o, *Decolonizing the Mind: The Politics of Language in African Literature,* reprint ed. (London: James Currey/Heinemann, 2011).

6   Kwame Anthony Appiah, "Is the Post- in Postmodernism the Post- in Postcolonial?," *Critical Inquiry* 17, no. 2 (1991): 336–57.

7   Ella Shohat, "Notes on the 'Post-Colonial,'" *Social Text,* no. 31/32 (1992): 99–113.

8   Perry Anderson, *Origins of Postmodernity* (New York: Verso, 1998).

9   The idea of a generation is extremely problematic in almost all circumstances. The circumstance of the baby boom does make the use of the concept pertinent here.

10   See Ihab Hassan, *The Postmodern Turn* (Columbus: Ohio University Press, 1987); Jencks, *Language of Postmodern Architecture*; Venturi et al., *Learning from Las Vegas.*

11   Jean-François Lyotard, *The Postmodern Condition: A Report on Knowledge,* trans. Geoff Bennington and Brian Massumi (1979;

repr., Minneapolis: University of Minnesota Press, 1984), xxiii.

12 Ibid., xxv.

13 Ibid., 65.

14 Ibid.

15 Anderson, *Origins of Postmodernity,* 58.

16 Ibid., 62.

17 Jameson, *Postmodernism,* xx.

18 Haraway, "A Cyborg Manifesto."

19 Gayatri Chakravorty Spivak, "Can the Subaltern Speak?," reprinted in her larger work *Critique of Postcolonial Reason: Toward a History of the Vanishing Present* (Cambridge, Mass.: Harvard University Press, 1999).

20 Haraway, "A Cyborg Manifesto," 150.

21 Ibid., 156.

22 Ibid., 176.

23 See Latour, *We Have Never Been Modern.*

24 Haraway, "A Cyborg Manifesto," 175.

25 Ibid., 176.

26 Spivak, "Can the Subaltern Speak?," 24.

27 Edward Said, *Orientalism* (New York: Vintage Books, 1979).

28 Ibid., 23.

29 Ibid., 37.

30 See Lionel Ruffel, "Un réalisme contemporain: les narrations documentaires," *Littérature* 166 (February 2012): 13–25.

31 Spivak, "Can the Subaltern Speak?," 50.

32 Ibid.

33 Ibid., 51.

34 Dipesh Chakrabarty, *Provincializing Europe: Postcolonial Thought and Historical Difference* (Princeton, N.J.: Princeton University Press, 2000).

35 Homi Bhabha, *The Location of Culture* (1994; repr., New York: Routledge Classics, 2004), 1.

36 Ibid., 6.

37 Latour, *We Have Never Been Modern,* 69.

38   Ibid., 74.
39   Ibid., 131.
40   Ibid., 48.
41   Michael Hardt and Antonio Negri, *Commonwealth* (Cambridge, Mass.: Harvard University Press, 2009), 114.
42   Ibid., 106.
43   Ibid., 110.
44   Ibid.
45   Ibid., 112.
46   Ibid., 113.
47   Ibid., 114.
48   Appadurai, *Modernity at Large.*
49   Emily Apter, *Against World Literature: On the Politics of Untranslatability* (London: Verso, 2013), 65.

FIFTH SERIES: INSTITUTIONS

1   Hal Foster, "Questionnaire on 'The Contemporary,'" *October* 130 (Fall 2009): 3.
2   Nancy Condee, Okwui Enwezor, and Terry Smith, eds., *Antinomies of Art and Culture: Modernity, Postmodernity, Contemporaneity* (Durham, N.C.: Duke University Press, 2008).
3   See Nicolas Bourriaud, ed., *Altermodern: Tate Triennial* (London: Tate, 2009).
4   Razmig Keucheyan, *The Left Hemisphere: Mapping Contemporary Theory,* trans. Gregory Elliott (2010; repr., London: Verso, 2013).
5   "What Is Contemporary Art?," *e-flux Journal,* no. 11 (December 2009), and "What Is Contemporary Art?," *e-flux Journal,* no. 12 (January 2010).
6   Hal Foster, "Contemporary Extracts," *e-flux Journal,* no. 12 (January 2010).
7   Cuauhtémoc Medina, "Contemp(t)orary: Eleven Theses," *e-flux Journal,* no. 12 (January 2010), para. 7.
8   Ibid.

9   See Immanuel Wallerstein, *World-Systems Analysis: An Intro-duction* (Durham, N.C.: Duke University Press, 2004).

10   Medina, "Contemp(t)orary: Eleven Theses," para. 10.

11   See Luc Boltanski and Ève Chiapello, *The New Spirit of Capital-ism* (London: Verso, 2007).

12   See Francesco Masci, *Entertainment! Apologie de la domination* (Paris: Allia, 2011).

13   See Pascale Casanova, "The Literary Greenwich Meridian: Some Thoughts on the Temporal Forms of Literary Belief," *Field Day Review* 4 (2008) : 7–23.

14   Guy Debord, *The Society of the Spectacle,* trans. Donald Nicholson-Smith (1967; repr., New York: Zone Books, 1994), 1.

15   Ibid., 155.

16   Jacques Rancière, *The Politics of Aesthetics: The Distribution of the Sensible,* trans. Gabriel Rockhill (London: Bloomsbury, 2004), 8.

17   Jacques Rancière, *The Emancipated Spectator,* trans. Gregory Elliott (London: Verso, 2009), 17.

18   Ibid., 19.

19   In this sense, it could be compared to another collective em-blematic of the era, the five Italian writers who formed the group Wu Ming.

20   See the Raqs Media Collective collection *Seepage* (Berlin: Stern-berg Press, 2010).

21   The Raqs Media Collective, "Additions, Subtractions: On Col-lectives and Collectivities," 3, http://www.raqsmediacollective.net/images/pdf/9e2537f1-e9e3-4849-956d-6f10b790b590.pdf.

22   See Chloe Nicolet-dit-Félix and Gulru Vardar, "Interview with Raqs Media Collective on the Exhibition, *Sarai Reader 09,*" *On Curating,* June 19, 2003, http://www.on-curating.org/issue-19-reader/interview-with-raqs-media-collective-on-the-exhi-bition-sarai-reader-09.html.

23   Previous issues of the *Sarai Reader* include 01, "The Public Domain"; 02, "The Cities of Everyday Life"; 03, "Shaping Tech-nologies"; 04, "Crisis/Media"; 05, "Bare Acts"; 06, "Turbulence";

07, "Frontiers"; and 08, "Fear." http://sarai.net/category/publica tions/sarai-reader/.

24   http://www.e-flux.com/announcements/33853/sarai-reader-09 -the-exhibition/.

25   See *Sarai Reader 09: Projections,* xi, http://archive.sarai.net/files /original/457a6e7bde8cd1b674b8cea8e94eedea.pdf.

26   Rancière, *Emancipated Spectator,* 49.

27   Transcribed in *Field Notes* 1 (April 2012): 91–106.

28   See Bill Ashcroft, Gareth Griffiths, and Helen Tiffin, *The Empire Writes Back: Theory and Practice in Post-Colonial Literature* (New York: Routledge, 1989).

29   "Has the Moment of the Contemporary Come and Gone?," 97.

30   Ibid., 98.

31   Ibid., 99.

32   Asia Art Archive, "About Us," http://www.aaa.org.hk/About /Overview.

33   Octavio Paz, *In Search of the Present: 1990 Nobel Lecture,* bilingual ed. (Fort Washington, Pa.: Harvest Books, 1991).

SIXTH SERIES: ARCHAEOLOGY

1   Miguel Valderrama, ed., *¿Qué es lo contemporáneo? Actualidad, tiempo histórico, utopias del presente* (Santiago, Chile: Universidad Finis Terrae, 2011).

2   Ibid., 8.

3   Ibid., 106.

4   Luis G. de Mussy, "Alfabetización histórica," in Valderrama, *¿Qué es lo contemporáneo?,* 123.

5   Henry Rousso, *The Latest Catastrophe: History, the Present, the Contemporary,* trans. Jane Marie Todd (Chicago: University of Chicago Press, 2016), 19.

6   Ibid., 3.

7   Ibid., 24.

8   Ibid., 28.

9   Patrick Boucheron, "L'entretien du monde," in *Pour une histoire-*

monde, ed. Patrick Boucheron and Nicolas Delalande (Paris: PUF, 2013), 18.

10 François Hartog, *Regimes of Historicity: Presentism and Experiences of Time,* trans. Saskia Brown (New York: Columbia University Press, 2015), 201.

11 Ibid., 9.

12 The final chapter in *Design and Crime (and Other Diatribes)* (London: Verso, 2002).

13 Here are Foster's two uses of the term: "Through formal transformation that is also social engagement, then, such work helps to restore a mnemonic dimension to contemporary art, and to resist the presentist totality of design in culture today" (ibid., 130). "Not so long ago, cinema was the medium of the future; now it is a privileged index of a recent past, and the fundamental element of a nonsynchronous protest against the presentist totality of the culture of design" (ibid., 139).

14 Georges Didi-Huberman, *Devant le temps: Histoire de l'art et anachronism des images* (Paris: Minuit, 2000), 15.

15 Thanks to Martin Rueff, "La concordance des temps," in Ruffel, *Qu'est-ce que le contemporain?,* 93–110.

16 Didi-Huberman, *Devant le temps,* 16.

17 Ibid., 103.

18 Ibid., 86.

19 Ibid.

20 Ibid., 102.

21 Ibid., 107.

22 Ibid., 108.

23 Laurent Olivier, *The Dark Abyss of Time: Archaeology and Memory,* trans. Arthur Greenspan (Lanham, Md.: Rowman and Littlefield, 2015), 188.

24 Paraphrased in accordance with the version the author references. For more on these concepts, see ibid., 75–105.—Trans.

25 Italics added.

26 See Georges Didi-Huberman, *Atlas, ou le Gai Savoir inquiet* (Paris: Minuit, 2001).

27   Michel Foucault, "Of Other Spaces: Utopias and Heterotopias,"
     trans. Jay Miskoweic, cited in Aliocha Imhoff and Kantuta
     Quirós, *Géoesthétique* (Paris: B42, 2014), 8.
28   See Manuel DeLanda, *A Thousand Years of Nonlinear History*
     (New York: Zone Books, 1997).
29   Stuart Hall, introduction to *Culture, Media, Language,* ed. Stuart
     Hall, Dorothy Hobson, Andrew Lowe, and Paul Willis (1980;
     repr., New York: Routledge, 2005), 4.
30   Raymond Williams, *Culture and Materialism: Selected Essays*
     (1980; repr., London: Verso, 2005), 47.
31   Hall, introduction, 7.
32   Ibid., 14–25.
33   Ibid., 3–7.
34   Ibid., 6.
35   Williams, *Culture and Materialism,* 41.
36   Ibid., 34.

CONCLUSION

1   Pireyre, "Fictions documentaires," 128.
2   Ibid., 125.
3   Didi-Huberman, *Devant le temps,* 103.
4   Latour, *We Have Never Been Modern,* 136.
5   Foucault, "Of Other Spaces," 1.
6   See Bernard Westphal, *La Géocritique: Réel, fiction, espace* (Paris:
    Minuit, 2007), and also Edward W. Soja, *Thirdspace: Journeys
    to Los Angeles and Other Real and Imagined Places* (Cambridge:
    Blackwell, 1996).

Index

Lionel Ruffel is head of department and professor of comparative literature at Université Paris 8.

Raymond N. MacKenzie has published translations of works by François Mauriac, Baudelaire, Flaubert, Zola, and Montesquieu as well as Barbey D'Aurevilly's *Diaboliques: Six Tales of Decadence* (Minnesota, 2015) and Stendhal's *Italian Chronicles* (Minnesota, 2017). He is professor of English at the University of St. Thomas in St. Paul, Minnesota.